Biblical Reflections
on the Eucharist

Precious Gifts

Biblical Reflections
on the Eucharist

JOHN F. CRAGHAN

Liguori
ONE LIGUORI DRIVE
LIGUORI MO 63057-9999

Imprimi Potest:
Harry Grile, CSsR, Provincial
Denver Province, The Redemptorists

Published by Liguori Publications
Liguori, Missouri 63057

To order, call 800-325-9521, or visit liguori.org

Library of Congress Cataloging-in-Publication Data

Craghan, John F.
  Precious gifts : biblical reflections on the Eucharist / by John F. Craghan.—1st ed.
    p. cm.
  ISBN 978-0-7648-2026-7
  1. Lord's Supper—Catholic Church—Meditations. 2. Bible—Theology—Meditations.
  3. Catholic Church—Prayers and devotions. I. Title.
  BX2215.3.C73 2011
  264'.36—dc23
                                    2011021154

Liguori Publications, a nonprofit corporation, is an apostolate of the Redemptorists. To learn more about the Redemptorists, visit Redemptorists.com.

Printed in the United States of America
15 14 13 12 11 / 5 4 3 2 1
First Edition

*For the Redemptorist community
throughout the world, especially the Baltimore Province,
in deep gratitude and appreciation for sharing with me
the rich legacy of Alphonsus*

CONTENTS

PREFACE

The title of this work was inspired by Matthew 13:44: "The kingdom of heaven is like treasure buried in a field, which a person finds and hides again, and out of joy goes and sells all that he has and buys that field." This parable, which is unique to Matthew, involves four stages. The first stage is the traditional work of a farmer where circumstances dictate a whole future. The second stage is about how finding the treasure opens up a new world. The third stage is a total reversal of the past that compels the farmer to sell everything he owns. The fourth and final stage is a new life for the farmer, with new possibilities grounded in the person of Jesus.

As I wrote this book, I thought especially of those Catholics who completed their formal religious education at the end of high school. Many such people seek to reconnect with their Catholic heritage. Like the farmer in the parable, they possess a treasure hidden in a field that they want to rediscover. They are anxious to explore its contents so that, like the farmer, they may enter a world of new possibilities rooted in the person of Jesus. It is my hope that this book will help them discover a new world by focusing on different dimensions of the treasure of faith.

I also envision those in the Rite of Christian Initiation of Adults (RCIA) process. I hope that the unfolding of this treasure may help their journey of faith. I also hope that Bible study groups may examine particular aspects of this inexhaustible treasure more closely. The Bible is not merely a rich heirloom, but a catalyst that urges believers to discover and rediscover ever old but new dimensions of their faith.

As both sacrament and sacrifice, the Eucharist possesses the unique ability to reflect the dynamism that can connect so many dimensions of Christian community life. It is a special symbol that expresses the challenges, rewards, and dangers of living out the Gospel. Ultimately, the Eucharist functions as a prism through which believers can evaluate their whole lives. To experience the Eucharist is to experience all the values of the Good News.

This work mines the riches of the biblical tradition and enables believers to view the Eucharist from a variety of vantage points. Hence, my use of ten biblical R's in the names of each chapter. The book attempts to enrich believers' understanding by considering various avenues to approach the Eucharist. Although I could have considered other biblical themes, I believe these ten themes serve as a beginning for reflection. In this way, Sunday Mass will emerge as a source of inspiration and encouragement for the week ahead, rather than another obligation. The treasure hidden in a field is ultimately a Eucharist that never ceases to arouse wonder and awe.

The format of each chapter is as follows. First, I suggest initial thoughts about the biblical theme stated in the chapter title. These may stem from human experience or other biblical passages. Second, I consider the biblical background as I examine scenes in both the Old and New Testaments. Third, I offer reflections on the theme and attempt to link them with the faith journey of the audience. Fourth, I deal with the Eucharist as it relates to the chapter theme and try to show

how it reveals a particular aspect of the Eucharist. Fifth, I recommend some review or discussion questions to explore the theme in greater depth.

I wish to thank my wife, Barbara Lynne Wenzel Craghan, for her advice and encouragement. She has provided insight from her own experience in both the classroom and parish ministry. Such insights have aided me in the selection and development of the Eucharist and ten biblical R's.

Finally, I dedicate this work to the Redemptorist community. As a young boy in the Redemptorist parish of Our Lady of Perpetual Help in Brooklyn, New York, I was first introduced to the rich theology of their founder, Saint Alphonsus de Liguori (1696–1787). In the years thereafter, the Redemptorists continued to help me absorb his teaching and attempt to make it accessible to others. This book is a small token of my enormous gratitude to them. May they continue to realize their motto of plentiful redemption.

JOHN F. CRAGHAN
AUGUST 1, 2010
—FEAST OF SAINT ALPHONSUS DE LIGUORI

CHAPTER ONE

Repentance

INITIAL THOUGHTS

In modern language, the word "repentance" evokes a considerable range of meaning. For some, it suggests the resolve to amend one's life and correct the errors of the past; therefore, it implies a certain dimension of regretting and deploring. For others, repentance may take on the added features of lament and bemoaning; here shame and reproach may play a vital role.

Repentance evokes the notion of change because of a new focus. Life is a journey, a quest for a particular object or goal through the reorientation of a person's ways. This object or goal may include a person, for example, finding the ideal marriage partner. It may also involve honor and prestige, for instance, becoming the CEO of a significant company or corporation. It may simply imply becoming the biggest and the best in a particular field or endeavor. Usually a journey involves expending untold amounts of time and energy. If the goal or objective of the journey is deemed worthwhile, the physical and mental demands in attaining it appear inconsequential. Spiritual repentance is captured in the language of faith, and Christians find in the Scriptures the need for their own conversion.

BIBLICAL BACKGROUND

In the Old Testament Prophets section, repentance is best expressed in the verb "to return." It means a total reorientation, a complete shifting of values. One retraces one's steps and, as in the parable of the prodigal son, goes home to one's father (Luke 15:18). The prophet Hosea depicts Israel as stumbling in her sinfulness and urges, "Return, O Israel, to the LORD your God; you have stumbled because of your iniquity" (Hosea 14:2).

When Jeremiah describes the stubbornness of his people, he diagnoses it as turning away from God. "Why then do these people resist with persistent rebellion? Why do they cling to deception, refuse to turn back" (Jeremiah 8:5)? However, once the whole process of reorientation begins, the focus of that change can only be God. "If you return, Israel—oracle of the LORD—return to me" (4:1). Speaking to his compatriots from the northern kingdom, Jeremiah articulates both God's mercy and the proper dispositions. "Return, rebellious children! I will heal your rebellions. 'Here we are! We belong to you; for you are the LORD, our God'" (3:22).

Another term associated with repentance is "life" or "to live." As a theological category, "life" implies fellowship with God, the ability to dialogue with God, the feeling of ease in his presence, and closeness to God. Ezekiel, for example, demonstrates the centrality of the "life" dimension of repentance. He quotes his audience as saying, "Our crimes and our sins weigh us down; we are rotting away because of them. How can we survive" (33:10)? To this community deprived of homeland and hope and burdened with the consciousness of their sins, the prophet replies directly and energetically: "As I live—oracle of the LORD God—I swear I take no pleasure in the death of the wicked, but rather that they turn from their ways and live. Turn, turn from your evil ways! Why should you die, house of Israel" (33:11)?

Like a very practical pastoral theologian, Ezekiel preaches about the signs or indications of repentance. A series of works points to the change of heart in the guilty. "Returning pledges, restoring stolen goods, walking by the statutes that bring life, doing nothing wrong—they shall surely live; they shall not die" (33:15). This apparently wooden style of preaching had nostalgic overtones for his community. It recalled the entrance liturgy at the temple when the people were bidden by the priest to examine their consciences. Only after the demands of justice in particular had been met could they sojourn in the Lord's tent and dwell on his holy mountain. Only then could the priest cry, "Lift up your heads, O gates; be lifted, you ancient portals, that the king of glory may enter" (Psalm 24:7).

Implied in this Old Testament notion of repentance is the central role of faith. Two Hebrew roots capture the salient aspects of faith: (1) to be strong, firm and (2) to trust in, rely on. In Genesis 15:6, Abram, lacking all evidence or proof of God's promise of numerous descendants, believes the Lord. He is made strong by opening himself up to God. In Jeremiah 17:7, the prophet announces, "Blessed are those who trust in the LORD; the LORD will be their trust." From the biblical perspective, faith involves the acceptance of a person, in this case the person of the God of Israel. In other words, one grounds oneself in the person of God. Having accepted this person, one is thus prepared to accept what this person says or reveals. This priority of person over statement may be outlined in these three steps: (1) I believe you, (2) I believe in you, and (3) I am prepared to believe what you tell me.

As partners in the covenant relationship, God and Israel have sworn allegiance to each other and, therefore, expect reciprocal faithfulness. The people of Israel must then demonstrate their faithfulness through concrete actions. Obedience thereby becomes the measure or standard for assessing genuine repentance and true faith.

A key term for repentance in the New Testament is the Greek word *metanoia*. It implies a new way of thinking that impacts a new way of acting. One New Testament scholar has suggested translating the verb form "to repent" as "to screw one's head on right." The result of this new way of thinking is that the person becomes transformed. Such repentance is the hallmark of the preaching of John the Baptist. According to Mark 1:4 and Luke 3:3, he fearlessly proclaims "a baptism of repentance for the forgiveness of sins." In Matthew 3:2, the Baptist urges such repentance since the kingdom of heaven has come near. At the same time, the Baptist links this radical call to positive proofs of this interior change. "Produce good fruit as evidence of your repentance" (Matthew 3:8; see also Luke 3:7–14).

Jesus of Nazareth follows in the footsteps of the Baptist but connects the call to repentance with the necessity of faith: "Repent, and believe in the gospel" (Mark 1:15). Ultimately, the Good News comprises not only the message but also the person of Jesus. This transformation of one's life is thus grounded in his message and person.

In the Gospel of Luke, Jesus sees his mission as nothing short of the universal proclamation of repentance. Following the call of Levi, he firmly announces, "I have not come to call the righteous to repentance but sinners" (Luke 5:32). In speaking of certain tragic events in Galilee and Jerusalem that claimed many lives, Jesus goes on to insist that, unless his audience repents, they, too, will perish (13:3, 5). In the parables of the lost sheep (15:7) and the lost coin (15:10), heaven must break out in exuberant joy over the one sinner who repents.

In the Acts of the Apostles, Luke captures the twofold prophetic dimensions of conversion, namely turning from sin and a turning to God/Jesus. At Solomon's Portico, Peter understands the mission of Jesus as a blessing "by turning each of you from your evil ways" (3:26). Paul and Barnabas interpret the healing of a cripple at Lystra as the occasion "to turn from these idols to the living God" (14:15). Paul explains his own conversion and subsequent mission as a turning from darkness to light and a turning from the power of Satan to God (26:18). Conversion in Acts, therefore, as in the prophetic literature, involves the movement of turning from and turning to. While turning from may require only an instant, turning to requires an arduous journey that demands no small measure of perseverance.

Alone among the evangelists, Luke deliberately constructs his Gospel and his second volume (Acts of the Apostles) along the axis of a journey that will inexorably take Jesus from Galilee (Luke 9:51) to Jerusalem, the city of destiny (19:28), and the Christian message from Jerusalem to Rome, the end of the earth (see Acts 1:8 and 28:16). In Luke, this journey brooks no obstacles. Jesus' determination is quite simply unrelenting. "Yet I must continue on my way today, tomorrow, and the following day, for it is impossible that a prophet should die outside of Jerusalem" (Luke 13:33). According to Luke, Jesus' journey also impacts the disciples, since they must follow him on his way (9:57–62). Significantly, one of the names for this community of disciples is "the Way" (Acts 9:2 and 19:23).

Luke demonstrates the connection between the call of Levi and his subsequent banquet (Luke 5:27–39), and while Luke does not employ overt eucharistic language, he still makes abundantly clear how breaking bread with Jesus impacts one's radical commitment to reorient one's life. The great banquet hosted by Levi (v. 29) provokes more than dismay for the Pharisees and their scribes since the guest list includes a large crowd of tax collectors and others (v. 30). When the Pharisees ask Jesus' disciples why he associates with such people, Jesus himself responds, "I have not come to call the righteous to repentance but sinners" (v. 32).

REFLECTIONS

Repentance is a total turning away from everything that makes community with God and others impossible. In the Bible, it is often a turning away from idols and, therefore, allegiance to other gods. The image of idols still functions as a viable symbol today. Humans create their own idols, even though they may not label them as such. These idols masquerade as the energy-sapping and all-engaging forces of daily life. They include the unbridled quest for power and dominance, the insatiable drive for pleasures of various kinds, the pursuit of ego leading to the destruction of genuine community, the reduction of persons to things or objects, the belligerent refusal to forgive injuries, etc.

Repentance, then, is also an all-out turning to God. God does not become a substitute for any of the above idols. In repentance, God emerges as the only genuine being who can completely satisfy the yearnings of the human heart. This is God, who takes humans seriously. They become his covenant partners and must demonstrate covenantal faithfulness through the fruits of repentance. This is also the God who is pure love, one who recognizes human weakness but never ceases to call these partners to head back home. This is the God who derives limitless joy in the repentance of only one sinner.

THE EUCHARIST

The Eucharist is an event that profoundly expresses Jesus' call to conversion, a call that excludes no one. To celebrate this meal with Jesus means, among other things, to renew one's intent to reorient one's life by accepting Gospel values.

Modern believers face similar situations in their celebration of the Eucharist because they, too, encounter the dangers of elitism. The Eucharist only begins in the place of worship, but it continues to be acted out in daily life. Given these circumstances, repentance becomes the order of the day. Believers must undergo a change of values that will reorient their lives. Such repentance, in effect, means adopting the mind of Jesus and hence searching out and providing for the less fortunate. To obtain such a new scale of values and act upon them is to repent and recapture this aspect of the Eucharist.

In describing Jesus' insistence on repentance and faith in the Good News (1:15), Mark uses the present imperative in Greek ("repent and believe") that implies incomplete action. In others words, believers experience an incomplete agenda. In their lifetime, they are constantly involved in responding to Jesus' initial call. Each day they must renew their resolve to turn away from all those idols and turn to the one who alone can satisfy their genuine desires and longings. Jesus' audience must continue to repent and persevere in believing, which is a journey.

Journey conjures up the hazards and hardships that can impede any kind of progress. At the same time, it focuses attention on the ultimate goal, namely union with God and God's extended family. The journey image does not evoke scenes of isolated individuals doing "their own thing." Rather, it envisions a family of believers engaged in a common quest. The eucharistic journey, therefore, presumes the notion of community. The personal transformation involved in repentance has communal contours. To turn away from idols and turn to the living God implies traveling with the sisters and brothers of Jesus. Wherever family members journey, they are in the company of their brother, Jesus.

This is the God who has become incarnate in Jesus of Nazareth. He is the one who suffers pain with his followers but also laughs with them. He is the one humans cannot measure with their finite standards of calculation. He is the one who suffers the defection of Judas but welcomes the conversion of Peter. He is the one who dares to become present to human needs through the lives of others. Jesus reveals the God who balances what seem to be the mutually exclusive attributes of justice and love, core values at the heart of the Eucharist.

The penitential rite at the beginning of Mass plays a significant role in this interplay between the Eucharist and repentance. The rite vividly reminds participants that they are indeed sinners ever in need of forgiveness and compassion. In effect, the rite urges them to renew their intent to turn from sin and turn to God. It also recalls Jesus' statement at Levi's banquet that he has come to call sinners, not the righteous. Having acknowledged their failures, believers can proceed to receive the food and drink that will sustain them in their journey. The truly repentant always travels with more than adequate provisions.

REVIEW AND/OR DISCUSSION QUESTIONS

1. *Is repentance merely something cerebral, or is it more involved?*

2. *Is repentance a once-and-for-all event, or does it demand daily effort?*

3. *Does the image of a journey help in understanding the ongoing demands of repentance?*

4. *How are the Eucharist and repentance connected?*

CHAPTER TWO

Remission

INITIAL THOUGHTS

The Bible gives a profound understanding of sin, that is, a truly personal notion in which God and humans interact as offended and offender, respectively. It is within the relationship between Creator and creature that it is necessary to heal what can be broken, which makes the word "remission" appropriate.

"Remission" takes several directions. First, it suggests the notion of the cancellation or relinquishment of claims, debts, and the like. Thus, the person who experiences the remission of sins realizes that God or God's representative holds no claim against him or her. In a certain legal sense the person has been acquitted and released and so savors once again the joy of freedom.

Second, "remission" clearly articulates the act of pardoning or forgiving, hence the expression "the remission of sins." It is a movement whereby God or the community acting in God's name liberates the person or persons from the guilt and anxiety associated with sin. To that extent, therefore, remission makes one think of the regaining of prior liberty and reinstatement in God's good graces.

In the Bible, remission enjoys a much more positive role, for while the secular overtones of release from debt and fiscal reinstatement do not completely disappear, the religious values occupy center stage. The process of the remission of sins involves a ritual of cleansing and, ultimately, restoration.

BIBLICAL BACKGROUND

The ancient Israelites considered the human person as a totality, not the sum of his or her parts. This anthropology applies to such terms as "heart" and "spirit." In the Hebrew Bible, the heart is the mind and will rather than the seat of the emotions. The heart thus represents the whole person and serves as the source of all actions and loyalties. In turn, the spirit represents the entire person under God's influence, open to God's will, and ever prompt to obey.

There are three key Hebrew meanings of "to sin." One is "to be found deficient or miss a particular mark or goal." In its theological sense, it signifies the failure to perform one's duty toward God. A second Hebrew meaning is "to rebel." A third Hebrew meaning is "to be malformed, crooked, bent." In its theological use, this usage implies the moral guilt or iniquity that God observes. It establishes a connection between the reality of sin and subsequent guilt and punishment.

Psalm 51 (the *Miserere* from the initial word of the Latin translation) serves as an example of the personal nature of sin, the cleansing process of remission, and the reorientation or reinstatement of the sinner in God's good graces. Believers can derive enormous benefit by reflecting on these diverse elements. The psalm is nothing less than a paradigm for a genuine remission of sin.

Sensing the state of sin and its subsequent shame, the psalmist seeks a cleansing from God. One Hebrew activity for such cleansing is the washing of clothes in cold water, beating them against rocks, and working them over with wood ("thoroughly wash away my guilt" v. 4). In verse 7, he sees this divine washing as resulting in a whiteness beyond that of snow. A second Hebrew action for cleansing has cultic overtones. In verse 9, the psalmist petitions God to perform the act of ritual purification ("cleanse me with hyssop that I may be pure"). The outcome of this cultic act is that in verse 12 the psalmist pleads, "A clean heart create for me, God." Such a heart stands for a purified self-determination to follow a faithful course of action.

Verse 17 parallels a contrite spirit with a humbled and contrite heart. In verse 19, the psalmist remarks that God will not scorn a contrite and humbled heart. In other words, God will not spurn one who has turned around his or her life in the wake of catastrophe. In verse 14, he requests a willing spirit. The psalmist will emerge pure (v. 9). Such phrases reflect a person who, having suffered disaster, now regroups and enters upon an entirely new manner of life.

The Bible also articulates the notion of remission in the institutions of the sabbatical year and the jubilee year. The sabbatical year is the last of a cycle of seven years. The impetus for such a year was the alienation of family property and the growth of lending at interest that, in turn, led to an increase of pauperism in Israel and the enslavement of defaulting debtors or their dependents. The sabbatical year aimed at counteracting such social inequality. Accordingly, Deuteronomy 15:1–2 stipulates, "At the end of every seven-year period you shall have a remission of debts, and this is the manner of the remission. Creditors shall remit all claims on loans made to a neighbor...." According to Exodus 23:10–11, the Israelites may sow their land and gather in its yield, but in the seventh year the land is to lie fallow so that the poor may eat. The thrust of this legislation is justice for the poor and Sabbath rest.

The jubilee year took place every fifty years at the conclusion of seven weeks of years. According to Leviticus 25, there were several complex provisions: lands lying fallow, forfeited property returned, and debtors and slaves set free. Remission and liberation are closely related. The jubilee year, in parallel with the sabbatical year, represented a type of solemn homecoming that celebrated liberation from severe economic conditions. It was indeed fitting that the homecoming should be announced by a blast of the ram's horn (Leviticus 25:9). Although the fields were to lie fallow, the jubilee year placed greater emphasis on overturning the poverty and misery that made life truly unbearable. To that extent, remission becomes synonymous with liberation.

It is not only the legal portion of the Old Testament that discusses the jubilee year. At least one prophetic passage makes the same eloquent appeal. An anonymous prophet or group of prophets, known as Third Isaiah, preached a message of hope for the very desperate in Judah and Jerusalem, "The spirit of the LORD God is upon me....He has sent me to bring good news to the afflicted, to bind up the brokenhearted, To proclaim liberty to the captives, release to the prisoners, To announce a year of favor from the LORD" (Isaiah 61:1–2). This anonymous figure presents himself as the human agent the Lord has designated to execute his transformative work for a discouraged and forlorn community. The proclamation of a jubilee year is nothing short of astonishing news and becomes an element of Jesus' message.

This is evidenced by Jesus' inaugural sermon in the Nazareth synagogue, as Luke says in his Gospel. Combining Isaiah 61:1–2 with Isaiah 58:6, he makes a programmatic statement about his mission, with obvious emphasis on remission and liberation. Having unrolled the prophetic scroll, he announces the focus of his ministry with this passage: "The Spirit of the Lord is upon me, because he has anointed me to bring glad tidings to the poor. He has sent me to proclaim liberty to captives and recovery of sight to the blind, to let the oppressed go free, and to proclaim a year acceptable to the Lord" (4:18–19). In short, Jesus views his entire mission as nothing less than a jubilee year. He boldly declares that this passage is fulfilled in his very person.

Earlier in Luke's Gospel, Zechariah describes the ministry of his son in these words: "to give his people knowledge of salvation through the forgiveness of their sins" (Luke 1:77). Thus, the Baptist will announce the coming salvation in Jesus, whose ministry will cause the remission of sins. Both Mark 1:4 and Luke 3:3 characterize John's baptism as one of "repentance for the forgiveness of sins." Hence, the purpose of his baptism of repentance is the remission of sins. In the parable of the prodigal son (Luke 15:11–32), the image of the homecoming banquet captures the overwhelming joy linked to the forgiveness of sins. In the account of the sinful woman (7:36–50) the remission of sins results in a peace (v. 50) that she did not previously enjoy. The healing of the paralytic demonstrates Jesus' ability to forgive sins and provokes awe and amazement on the part of the witnesses (Matthew 9:2–8, Mark 2:1–12, and Luke 5:17–26).

In John 20:23, the Easter gift of the Risen One to the fearful disciples is the power to forgive sins. "Behold the Lamb of God, who takes away the sin of the world" (1:29)! (In 1:36, John again designates Jesus as the Lamb of God but omits "who takes away the sin of the world.") The title "lamb" has generated a variety of interpretations: (1) the conquering lamb who overcomes evil in the world (see Revelation 17:14), (2) the suffering servant who is led like a sheep to the slaughter and remains silent like a lamb before its shearers (Isaiah 53:7), and (3) the Passover lamb whose blood applied to the door-posts of the Israelites assures their deliverance (Exodus 12:22).

While these views all have their merits, perhaps it is more helpful to set the "Lamb of God" title against the background of Israel's sacrificial rites (especially the sin and the guilt offerings). Their purpose is to reestablish union with God after the commission of sin. In using this title, the author of John underscores Jesus as the Lamb of God who comes from the Father with the mission of overcoming the world's sin. Far from being a cultic victim, Jesus thus transcends all such sacrifices. By laying his life down on the cross, Jesus takes away the world's sin.

Following in the line of Jesus, Paul will make remission of sins through baptism a cornerstone of his preaching. Baptism as a cleansing that pardons sin plays a central role in Paul's authentic letters and those attributed to him. In 1 Corinthians 6:11, Paul connects the baptismal washing with sanctification and justification. The cleansing action of baptism means incorporation into Christ. "For all of you who were baptized into Christ have clothed yourselves with Christ" (Galatians 3:27). Ephesians 5:26 attests that Christ makes the Church holy by "cleansing her by the bath of water with the word." Titus 3:5 speaks of rebirth and renewal by the Holy Spirit. Through the cleansing action of the waters of baptism, therefore, believers have all their sins forgiven, are incorporated into Christ, and are dedicated to God.

REFLECTIONS

While sin is a personal denial to accept God's will for well-being, it also has social repercussions. Perhaps no one grasped the social notion of sin better than Paul in 1 Corinthians. There he views the Christian community as a single body composed of many members (see 12:12–31). Actually, Christians are members of Christ himself. In this passage, Paul exhorts his Corinthian converts to use their gifts and talents for the common good. By incorporation into Christ, believers become interdependent, not independent. The action of one member naturally affects the whole community. In addressing the issue of casual sex with a prostitute (6:12–20), Paul emphasizes the significance of the body as a temple of the Holy Spirit and adds that believers are not their own. In sinning, therefore, the Corinthians flaunt their independence to the detriment of the rest of the community. Briefly put, sin has social significance for Paul, who understands the human capacity to sin in the members of the early communities.

THE EUCHARIST

To celebrate the Eucharist is to recapture the mind of Jesus, who opposes everything that oppresses and depresses the human spirit. Such oppression and depression are often coupled with the burden of human sinfulness. The eucharistic Jesus presents himself as one who, through his self-giving, dismantles the shackles of sins and through his Church invites all overburdened believers to heed his invitation, "Come to me, all you who labor and are burdened, and I will give you rest" (Matthew 11:28). Matthew describes Jesus as one who will take away the burden of sin.

Matthew's Gospel, written around twenty years after Paul's death, sets the institution of the Eucharist in the midst of the wavering disciples who would turn their backs on the leader. In 26:14–15, he portrays Judas as the one who will betray Jesus to the chief priests for financial compensation. In 26:20–25, Jesus announces that one of the Twelve will betray him. After the institution of the Eucharist (26:26–30a), Jesus solemnly declares in 26:30b–35 that all his disciples will desert him. Although Peter pledges his undying fidelity, Jesus must painfully inform him that he will deny his master no less than three times. As the scene concludes, all the other disciples profess their wholehearted loyalty. Hence, it is ironic that the institution of the Eucharist in Matthew for the remission of sins includes the betrayer, the denier, and all the deserters who are actually sharing this meal with Jesus. In this scene, therefore, Matthew powerfully reminds his community that the remission of sins also extends to the leaders.

Addressing his community where sin and forgiveness is a central issue (see 18:15–35), Matthew makes it abundantly clear that disciples can experience remission because of the Eucharist. Here forgiveness does not depend on fidelity or obedience. Rather, it stems from Jesus' sacrifice that is symbolized in the Eucharist. Forgiveness of sins is nothing less than a gift from the self-giving Jesus. Matthew's emphasis on the Eucharist for the precise purpose of forgiving sins would evoke those biblical images associated with it. Forgiveness brings immediately to mind the notion of liberty or freedom. The remission of sins means that one has broken free from the stranglehold of servitude. It also reminds one of healing. The sinner once wracked with guilt receives a healing that encompasses his or her whole person. It also recalls the gift of peace. The liberated and healed person is now prepared to rejoin the community and set aside all those obstacles that obstructed genuine peace.

The Gospel associations with remission merit consideration. In the parable of the prodigal son, the atmosphere of exuberant joy pervades the entire account, with the exception of the pouting elder son. The emotionally unrestrained father demands celebration because his younger son was dead and is alive, was lost and is now found. In the account of the sinful woman, the host inwardly excoriates her, implying that she is a scarlet woman. After his exchange with the host about the relationship of creditors and debtors, Jesus dismisses the woman with, "go in peace" (Luke 7:50). With the remission of sins comes an unfathomable peace.

At Mass, we say, "Behold the Lamb of God, behold him

who takes away the sin of the world," viewing Jesus' mission through the eyes of John. Jesus transcends all liturgical offerings. It is now Jesus' own blood, not the blood of the lamb, that makes the remission of sins possible. By offering himself on Calvary, Jesus fulfills his mission as the Lamb of God. Having entered human history at the Father's command, he now takes away the sin of the world precisely through his death. Once again, it is death that makes the new life of pardon possible.

At the Easter Vigil, the premier eucharistic celebration of the Church year, candidates for baptism personally experience the fulfillment of this inaugural sermon. In baptism they encounter release or freedom from the oppression of their sins. In the transforming waters of the sacrament, they share in the spirit of Jesus that continues to make jubilee years possible. The prophet from Nazareth energizes them through the work of this spirit to emerge from the waters of baptism as reborn, renewed, and liberated. By consuming his Body and Blood, the faithful take up their role in furthering the work of the kingdom, and they experience firsthand that remission has become synonymous with freedom.

REVIEW AND/OR DISCUSSION QUESTIONS

1. *How does the Old Testament express the personal nature of sin?*

2. *How does Luke describe the mission of Jesus in his inaugural sermon (4:16–30)?*

3. *How does Paul understand the social nature of sin?*

4. *How do the letters of Paul describe baptism as a washing or cleansing?*

CHAPTER THREE

Redemption

INITIAL THOUGHTS

A pawnshop can often be the setting for an understanding of redemption. People have to surrender an item because of circumstances. They receive a low price for an item, then buy it back or "redeem" it when their circumstances improve. As a result, redemption becomes merely buying and selling. It can be difficult for people to see a higher order at work in this tedious task of redemption. Consequently, redemption appears condemned to a meaningless existence at the edge of their theological world.

It is also tempting to regard redemption as a *fait accompli*.

Something occurred in the distant past and that something continues to have an impact on the present. Redemption is thereby reduced to an open-and-shut case. The Redeemer has carried out his mission—Jerusalem has spoken and so the issue is resolved.

For many believers, the cross has lost its power as a symbol. It no longer evokes the irony and the authority it originally possessed. It has become relegated as a common icon on traditional church furniture and has ceased to receive the attention that Paul poignantly describes for his Corinthian converts. "For Jews demand signs and Greeks look for wisdom, but we proclaim Christ crucified, a stumbling block to Jews and foolishness to Gentiles, but to those who are called, Jews and Greeks alike, Christ the power of God and the wisdom of God" (1 Corinthians 1:22–24). For Paul, there is no shortcut around Calvary. To speak of redemption is to speak of a Jesus who radiates power and wisdom through the weakness and folly of the cross.

All too often, redemption strikes believers as heavy theological jargon that no longer appeals to their imagination, similar to words such as salvation, justification, expiation, etc. The irony of this position is that it neglects the sociological background of the term, namely the redeemer as a family member who comes to the aid of distraught and often financially strapped relatives. To appreciate Jesus as Redeemer, we must first view him with an extended family of hurting relatives.

Incarnation, ministry, crucifixion, death, resurrection, ascension, exaltation, and Second Coming have become isolated, disconnected components in the plan of salvation. For example, many believers maintain that they are saved solely by the death of Jesus, not his resurrection. In other words, they have refused to see the separate elements forming a meaningful whole. They do not perceive the interdependence of these different phases. However, to hail Jesus as a redeemer is to form an image of him from the moment of entering human history to his return in glory at the end. Redemption does not remain a splintered, fragmented moment.

BIBLICAL BACKGROUND

The family setting provides the initial context for understanding redeemer and redemption. The redeemer is a family member, often the next of kin, who must rally to the aid of disadvantaged relatives. In Deuteronomy 19:4–6, the redeemer functions as the avenger of blood who retaliates against a perpetrator to preserve family honor in the case of homicide. When an Israelite is forced to sell himself or herself to an alien, any family member may redeem them by paying an appropriate purchase price (Leviticus 25:47–50). In the Book of Ruth, Boaz assumes the obligation of redemption when he agrees to purchase the property of Elimelech, Ruth's deceased husband, and thus keep it in the family (4:3–6). He also consents to marry Ruth "in order to raise up a family for her late husband" (4:10). Similarly, the prophet Jeremiah purchases the property of his cousin, Hanamel, at the direction of the Lord. "Purchase my field in Anathoth, since you, as nearest relative, have the first right of purchase" (Jeremiah 32:7).

In the Book of the Covenant, Exodus, 21:1—23:33, there is the bold statement, "You shall give me the firstborn of your sons. You must do the same with your oxen and your sheep" (22:28–29). Exodus 13:1–2 and 11–16, however, interprets the legal requirement. In place of the firstborn, Israel is to offer a substitute. The reason given is, "When Pharaoh stubbornly refused to let us go, the LORD killed every firstborn in the land of Egypt, from firstborn of human being and beast alike. That is why I sacrifice to the LORD every male that opens the womb, and why I ransom every firstborn of my sons" (Exodus 13:15). The Lord values the lives of the Israelites because they are his sons. Redemption is thus person-oriented.

The prophet of the exile, Isaiah, also uses the redemption theme to advantage. In his effort to reassure his despondent audience, he unequivocally states that God has obliterated their sins. Moreover, the one who forgives them is their redeemer, a family member, who rescues them from their dire predicament. "I have brushed away your offenses like a cloud, your sins like a mist; return to me, for I have redeemed you" (44:22). This redemptive intervention has geographical overtones. Recalling God's involvement at the Red Sea, Isaiah proclaims that this redeemer dried up that body of water and is now making "the depths of the sea into a way for the redeemed to pass through" (51:10).

In both Matthew 20:28 and Mark 10:45, Jesus' mission is interpreted as one of serving, not being served, and of giving his life as a ransom or redemption for many. This notion of ransom or redemption recalls the suffering servant in Isaiah who "surrendered himself to death... (and) bore the sins of many" (53:12). Jesus' self-giving in death is an act of redemption or liberation on behalf of humanity. While Luke does not use this saying from his source, Mark, he does employ the notion of redemption on several occasions. In his canticle, Zechariah sings of the Lord God of Israel who "visited and brought redemption to his people" (Luke 1:68). In the temple, the prophetess Anna praises God and speaks about the child

Jesus to all those awaiting the redemption of Jerusalem (2:38). The forlorn travelers on the road to Emmaus tell their new companion that they placed their hopes in Jesus as one who would redeem Israel (24:21). Jesus must then explain how all the recent events fulfilled God's plan in the Scriptures.

Paul develops the image of redemption in greater depth in his letters. Borrowing from the commercial world, where buying and selling were everyday activities, he interprets the self-giving of Jesus in death as an act of redemption in his Letter to the Galatians. Avoiding any mention of a purchase price or a recipient of the price, he writes, "Christ ransomed us from the curse of the law by becoming a curse for us" (3:13). In the next chapter, Paul observes that God sent his Son, born under the law, "to ransom those under the law, so that we might receive adoption" (4:5). Paul dwells on the curse inherent in crucifixion, since anyone so executed brings a curse on himself and defiles the land (see Deuteronomy 21:22–23). By his crucifixion, Jesus then becomes accursed. However, Paul adds that he becomes a curse for the sake of humanity. For Paul, therefore, Christ performs the role of kinsman who buys back enslaved or captive relatives. Jesus' suffering and death by crucifixion liberate sinners from bondage and enslavement. The scandal of the cross reveals the depth of God's redeeming love.

Other New Testament letters expand the notion of redemption. In Ephesians 1:7, Jesus' redemption through his blood makes possible the forgiveness of sins (see also Colossians 1:14). The personal dimension of Jesus' self-giving emerges in two other passages. In Titus 2:14, Jesus "gave himself for us to deliver us...a people as his own." The author of Hebrews situates Jesus' act of redemption on the Day of Atonement when he enters the Holy of Holies with his very own blood to obtain eternal redemption (9:12). In these passages, redemption highlights Jesus' outreach in death to the vulnerable and disenfranchised members of his extended family. The value of such members confirms the dictum that Jesus' blood is thicker than water.

··· 🍷 ···

REFLECTIONS

Family involvement must heighten believers' appreciation of the significance of redemption. The Exodus from Egypt, the pivotal event in Israel's relationship with God, is grounded in the kinship bond between these two parties. The Lord feels compelled to intervene on Israel's behalf. "I will redeem you by my outstretched arm..." (Exodus 6:6). Family honor requires divine involvement. The Lord's compassionate display of kinship in the Exodus serves as a powerful backdrop for the self-giving ministry of Jesus. Seeing distraught humanity wallowing in moral, physical, and emotional bondage, Jesus the kinsman must seek to liberate such despairing family members. In this instance, family honor becomes synonymous with the cross. Jesus interprets redemption as a total surrender in death for his sisters and brothers.

Redemption must not be reduced to vague theological jargon. Rather, it must regain a meaningful existence by absorbing the biblical images. One such strong image is blood. As the author of Hebrews states, Jesus approaches the Holy of Holies on Good Friday with his own blood, not that of animals. A second image is family orientation. Jesus is our redemption (1 Corinthians 1:30) who gives himself for us (Titus 2:14). As Redeemer, Jesus does not envision himself as suffering and dying for an anonymous and amorphous public. On the contrary, he sees himself in the tradition of his Bible as a latter-day suffering servant. Ultimately, Calvary reveals the insatiable demands of kinship.

This biblical understanding must transform and energize believers' notion of the cross. They must begin by fathoming its profound, scandalous nature. Roman citizens were not usually executed this way—crucifixion was generally reserved for low life. Yet Paul insists that he must proclaim Christ crucified. Though crucifixion is a scandal to the Jews and utter folly to the gentiles, Christ is thereby "the power of God and the wisdom of God" (1 Corinthians 1:24). Paul demands that Corinthian converts grasp this upsetting yet enriching notion of the cross. Against this background of redemption as intervention on the part of kin, today's believers must reassess their initial feelings of revulsion in considering the cross as the Roman means of capital punishment. Ironically, they must value it as a family treasure since it captures both the height and the depth of family devotion and involvement.

To a certain extent, redemption overlaps with liberation. In its biblical setting, enslaved family members are released from bondage and once again breathe the intoxicating air of freedom. The self-giving of Jesus in death becomes a liberating experience whereby he restores human dignity and a sense of renewed humanity to sisters and brothers. They regain their rightful position as family members and, having been thus exonerated, they sense that they must live up to the family name. To experience redemption means to share it with others.

This sharing of redemption with others implies that redemption is an open-ended, ongoing process. Admittedly, Jesus has already achieved redemption. However, the effects of his action centuries ago must impact family members today. This impact involves three steps. First, believers must recognize that, as redeemed sisters and brothers of Jesus, they must relate to his extended family. Second, they must become aware of the plight, problems, and catastrophes that this extended family encounters. Third, they must take positive steps to alleviate their difficulties. Hence all believers must follow the intrepid example of Jesus their brother and experience "the sharing of his sufferings by being conformed to his death" (Philippians 3:10).

THE EUCHARIST

According to Matthew, Mark, and Luke, the Last Supper with its institution of the Eucharist commemorated the Jewish feast of Passover. Originally, this was the feast of seminomadic shepherds who celebrated this ritual for the welfare of their flocks when the tribe set out for new pasture grounds. This was a very critical time in the life of the flock since young sheep and goats would then be born. Israel interpreted this ancient feast by adapting it to its own experience of God. It no longer involved the quest for a temporary pasture but for the final pasture, namely the Promised Land itself. In celebrating this feast, Israel recalled how their God had intervened on their behalf by defeating Pharaoh and his military forces. As Israel's warrior, God made good his earlier promise that he would redeem them with an outstretched arm and powerful acts of judgment (Exodus 6:6). After the Lord's stunning victory at the sea, they fittingly sang, "In your love you led the people you redeemed" (Exodus 15:13).

Against this Passover background, the celebration of the

Eucharist underlines Jesus' role as redeemer. By sacrificing himself, he makes possible the new trek, not from Egypt to the Promised Land, but from death to life. Ironically, it is Jesus' death that makes such life possible. In 1 Corinthians 5:8, Paul presents the death of Jesus in this Passover setting. "For our paschal lamb, Christ, has been sacrificed." The Eucharist, therefore, commemorates the gaining of freedom and hence life for Jesus' extended family. At the same time, the Eucharist challenges this family to emulate their kinsman by giving all of themselves to God. Redemption exacts a high price: one that the celebration of the Eucharist vividly portrays.

Mark's account of the institution of the Eucharist at the Last Supper (14:22–25), with the significant words "took... blessing...broke...gave" (v. 22), reminds his audience of the earlier feeding stories about the five thousand (6:30–44) and the four thousand (8:1–10). Now, however, Jesus chooses to share himself, his own Body and Blood, with his disciples. "This is my body" (v. 22) captures the destiny of Jesus, who will be handed over to death. However, this is a death for others that recalls Jesus' earlier saying that he came "to serve and to give his life as a ransom for many" (10:45). Seen from the sociological perspective, Jesus' self-giving is essentially an act of ransom or redemption on behalf of family members.

In the words over the cup, Jesus uses the expression "my blood of the covenant" (Mark 14:24). This evokes the blood rite performed by Moses on Mount Sinai. After the people promise to keep the terms of the covenant, Moses sprinkles blood on them, saying, "This is the blood of the covenant which the LORD has made with you" (Exodus 24:8). Since blood symbolizes life, Jesus is implying that the covenant or relationship between him and his community is ratified in his blood. By drinking from the cup (Mark 14:23), the disciples signal their willingness to share Jesus' destiny. Jesus then adds that this blood of the covenant "will be shed for many" (v. 24). The phrase recalls the fate of the suffering servant in Isaiah, specifically his atoning death for others (see Isaiah 53:12). The destiny of the suffering servant, Jesus, and his disciples is clearly intertwined.

These words of institution in Mark must resonate with today's followers of Jesus. Here Jesus, the kinsman, symbolizes the demands of redemption. His esteem and love for his extended family are such that he offers himself in death to solidify the bonds of covenant that join him to his sisters and brothers. This self-giving in death must prompt believers to see their own lives as one of serving and a ransom/redemption for many (Mark 10:45). According to Paul, in eating the bread and drinking the cup, believers "proclaim the death of the Lord" (1 Corinthians 11:26). In other words, believers must translate Jesus' manner of dying into their own manner of living. The criterion, therefore, is the shocking criterion of the cross, namely generous service to others. Jesus continues to have sisters and brothers who need the help of other family members, namely other redeemers.

REVIEW AND/OR DISCUSSION QUESTIONS

1. *In what ways does God function as redeemer in the Old Testament?*

2. *How does Paul apply the notion of redemption to Jesus?*

3. *In what ways does the New Testament depict Jesus' personal involvement in redemption?*

4. *How should believers appreciate the symbol of the cross against the background of redemption?*

CHAPTER FOUR

Reconciliation

INITIAL THOUGHTS

A first thought may be to dismiss reconciliation rather blandly and regard it as having little relevance to today's world. In this mindset, reconciliation assumes very impersonal contours. It may be reduced to the governmental practice of reconciliation. In this form, the Senate bill must be reconciled with the House of Representatives bill. While opposing issues may be found in both bills, they can be somewhat conveniently reconciled.

On second thought, the issue of reconciliation presents an entirely different face when human relationships are involved.

Everyone is well aware of people, including relatives and friends, who no longer speak to each other. The atmosphere of enmity and hatred seems to remove the "offending" party from actual existence. An edict of personal excommunication prevails. It is apparent to everyone that ego has created such a chasm that all human interaction is effectively severed.

All believers must contend with the reality of evil. It is simply inadequate to recognize the face of evil in the awkward gentleman with the red tights and protruding horns who appears every Halloween. To appreciate the immense power of sin, one need only peruse the daily papers or watch the news on television. Unfortunately, the power of evil wears many disguises so that people often fail to label it appropriately. An extramarital affair is labeled an indiscretion, and getting caught after stealing company funds is described as a business transaction gone awry. To recognize evil and counteract it pose formidable challenges for all believers.

Given the manifold presence of evil, how does Jesus combat its powerful grip on humanity? In other words, how does Jesus wrestle with the powers and principalities (Romans 8:38) that threaten to crush people and make genuine humanity impossible? For Paul, Jesus sets out to reconcile humanity to God through the cross. In this way, people become God's intimates and enjoy his friendship. The cross symbolizes Christ's victory over all inhuman powers that threaten to destroy God's creation.

BIBLICAL BACKGROUND

Mutual forgiveness figures prominently in the ministry of Jesus. In addition to the petition in the Lord's Prayer (see Matthew 6:12 and Luke 11:4), this obligation appears elsewhere in Jesus' teaching. Immediately after the Lord's Prayer, Matthew presents mutual forgiveness as the condition for God's pardon. "If you forgive others their transgressions, your heavenly Father will forgive you" (6:14). In developing the notion of anger as a violation of the commandment not to kill, Jesus offers sound advice. If, in offering a gift at the altar, one recalls that a sister or brother has something against the person, then the proper procedure is: (1) to leave the gift at the altar; (2) to go and be reconciled with the sister or brother; and (3) to return to offer the gift (Matthew 5:23–24). When Peter attempts to set limits (seven times) to forgiving a member of the community, Jesus responds, "Not seven times but seventy-seven times" (Matthew 18:22; also see Luke 17:4). In Matthew's parable of the unforgiving servant, the first servant who is forgiven a boundless debt refuses to forgive a fellow servant a relatively paltry debt. The parable concludes with Jesus' admonition, "So will my heavenly Father do to you (torture unless the debt is paid), unless each of you forgives his brother from his heart" (18:35).

As Paul assesses the world, he sees it caught in the grips of unbridled ego that often expresses itself in violent hostility. In Romans 1:18 to 3:20, Paul depicts both pagans and Jews as festering in this lamentable situation. A first cause of this condition is the separation of pagans from Israel (see Ephesians 2:11–12). A second cause is flesh, that is, the total human person wallowing in a history of sin and bent solely upon pursuit of self (see Romans 8:5–7). Paul personifies sin as he develops his theology of sin. Sin is thus a force and power unleashed upon the world since the commission of the first sin. By nature demonic, sin rules as a monarch (5:14 and 21) and pays wages (6:23) to bring about death, namely the loss of communal life with God. Concretely, sin reveals itself as a falling away from God's will, transgression, and an unwillingness to hear and comply (5:12–21).

Given this disarray, Paul emphasizes the achievement of Jesus' death and resurrection as nothing less than reconciliation. For them, resurrection means the restoration of humans and their world to a status of friendship with God and fellow humans. The underlying Greek root for reconciliation means "other" and denotes "making otherwise." It is rightly identified as atonement, or, "at-one-ment." They borrow this vocabulary from the Greco-Roman world where, in its secular sense, it marks a change or alteration of relationship between individual persons or groups of persons like nations. It reflects a profound change from anger, enmity, or hostility to love, friendship, or intimacy. Employing this term in a religious sense, Paul describes God as bringing about reconciliation with estranged humans through his Son. The outcome of this process is that, once they accept Christ, the former sinners enjoy a relationship of intimacy and love.

Paul underlines three aspects of reconciliation. First, Jesus' death brings about this reconciliation. "While we were enemies, we were reconciled to God through the death of his Son..." (Romans 5:10). The image of Jesus' blood captures the bond between him and those reconciled, "and through him to reconcile to all things for him, making peace by the blood of his cross" (Colossians 1:20). Second, reconciliation creates a world of peace that obliterates all those obstacles dividing Jews and gentiles as well as humans in general and God. "For he is our peace, he who made both one and broke down the dividing wall of enmity, through his flesh" (Ephesians 2:14). Third, reconciliation impacts the entire created universe. "God was reconciling the world to himself in Christ" (2 Corinthians 5:19). Just as the Spirit functions as the transforming agent in the lives of humans, that same Spirit also serves as the transforming agent in the material universe.

REFLECTIONS

Mutual forgiveness remains an essential imperative for all believers. Human ego is all too often brittle, frail, and fragile. It all too easily adopts a retaliatory mode in the face of injury, insult, or misunderstanding. In this impasse, believers must invoke the presence of the reconciling Jesus who prayed on the cross, "Father, forgive them, they know not what they do" (Luke 23:34). It's important to look beyond personal hurt and pain to hear Jesus' demand to experience the transforming power of Jesus' death. To say, "I forgive you" is but another way of saying, "I love you."

Like Paul, modern believers must also assess the causes of hostility in their world. To be sure, newspapers and television reports reveal that disunity and disharmony are more apparent than unity and harmony. Believers constantly hear of divisions, such as those between Sunnis and Shiites in the Muslim world, Tutsis and Hutus in Rwanda, and Catholics and Protestants in Northern Ireland. Closer to home, there is an ever-widening rift between the institutional Church and the laity. Not infrequently, there are breaches between husband and wife, as well as parents and family. Here, too, the cause is flesh, namely humans divorced from genuine concern for others and isolated in their own worlds of self-aggrandizement and exploitation. To borrow from Galatians 5, it is obvious that these are the works of the flesh, not the fruits of the spirit.

Believers must conclude that Paul's assessment of his world is alive and well in their own.

How should believers react to their world and causes of hostility? Clearly they must reject the ego-pursuing tendencies of sinful humans and adopt the actions of Jesus. Paul teaches his converts that they can find Jesus' lifestyle by reflecting on his death-style. "We were reconciled to God through the death of his Son" (Romans 5:10). Indeed Paul goes so far as to say that he has incorporated this death-style into his own lifestyle. "Be imitators of me, as I am of Christ" (1 Corinthians 11:1). For Paul the Jew, the mission to the gentiles symbolizes the breakdown of hostilities in his very own person. The genuine humanity of Jesus remains the only way to offset the view of fallen humanity espoused by so many.

In 2 Corinthians 5:18, Paul speaks of Christ in a twofold way: (1) God has reconciled humanity to himself through Christ and (2) has given believers the ministry of reconciliation. In Galatians 3:28, Paul describes the results of his ministry. "There is neither Jew nor Greek, there is neither slave nor free person, there is not male and female." In the light of these programmatic statements, believers must reflect their ministry of reconciliation by the overthrow of all those barriers that divide humanity.

With regard to ethnic origin (Jew or Greek), believers must work to bring about the death of blind nationalism and the exploitation of other peoples. They announce the fulfillment of reconciliation when truly human standards of living oppose the acquisition of wealth at the expense of others. With regard to the social status of slave or free, they must break down barriers by sharing their financial surplus with the helpless poor and, where possible, make them fiscally independent by providing jobs. With regard to gender, they must reject all forms of male chauvinism. By recognizing the talents and gifts of women and utilizing them to the full, male believers carry out the mandate of Galatians 3:28.

In considering the Pauline effects of reconciliation, believers, by their focus on the death of Jesus, must realize that reconciliation can be achieved only at the cost of immense effort. Paul's teaching endorses the need for patience. Paul's linking of reconciliation to peace must mean more than the cessation of hostilities. Peace includes the will to enjoy God's world/their world, a world that is meaningless without other people. In view of the cosmic dimension of reconciliation, believers must relearn the truth that the non-human world is also sacred. Reconciliation demands that they cease to rape the earth and begin to appreciate it as another form of God's presence.

THE EUCHARIST

The feeding of the five thousand in Mark 6:30–44 and the feeding of the four thousand in Mark 8:1–10 have clear links to the celebration of the Eucharist with their vocabulary of taking, blessing, breaking, and giving. In structuring these two accounts, Mark has introduced a geographical component whereby the feeding of the five thousand takes place in Jewish territory and that of the four thousand in gentile territory. By means of this structure, Mark addresses a central concern in his community, namely the mission to the gentiles. In Mark 8:17–21 Jesus is compelled to upbraid his disciples for their lack of understanding about the two episodes. "Why do you conclude that it is because you have no bread? Do you not yet understand or comprehend? Are your hearts hardened" (v. 17)? When Jesus further questions them about the number of baskets of fragments, they reply that they gathered twelve baskets at the first feeding and seven at the second (vv. 19–20). The twelve baskets obviously symbolize the Jews (the twelve tribes of Israel) and the seven baskets the gentiles (a likely numerical reference to universalism).

In these two accounts, Mark combines the celebration of the Eucharist with the issue of reconciliation. In effect, Mark seeks to defuse the tensions between Jewish Christians and gentile Christians. Obviously deep alienation emerged at the Eucharist that only genuine reconciliation could heal. Mark is laboring to move this mixed community to reconciliation by focus on the one bread. The source of hope in this endeavor resides in the compassion of the reconciling Jesus. For Mark, the Eucharist must not only encourage reconciliation but become the very means by which it is accomplished.

In the celebration of the Eucharist, Paul also insists on the role of unity. In 1 Corinthians 11:17–34, he criticizes the Corinthian Christians for the sense of elitism that divides the rich from the poor. Elsewhere in this letter, he emphasizes the overriding significance of unity. Unity brings about "*koinonia*" or communion. Appealing to the symbolism of the loaf of bread, he writes, "The bread that we break, is it not a participation (*koinonia*) in the body of Christ? Because the loaf of bread is one, we though many, are one body for we all partake of the one loaf" (10:16-17). For Paul, the celebration of the Eucharist is calculated to foster unity, not shatter it. Reconciliation is how unity comes about where it is wanting.

For Paul, the death or self-giving of Jesus in the Eucharist is intimately linked to the very notion of reconciliation. First,

Jesus' death is the cause of reconciliation. "While we were enemies, we were reconciled to God through the death of his Son..." (Romans 5:10). The image of blood (Colossians 1:20, "by the blood of his cross") graphically depicts Jesus' self-giving in death. Second, reconciliation creates a world of peace, "For he (Jesus) is our peace" (Ephesians 2:14). Third, reconciliation touches the entire cosmos, not just humans (2 Corinthians 5:19).

The celebration of the Eucharist impacts the involvement of believers on several levels of reconciliation. One level is reconciliation with the local community. To erect barriers of hate and then proceed to the table of love is a contradiction. Another level is reconciliation with national communities and even the world. To take part in the Eucharist is to proclaim the self-giving of Jesus and hence the overthrow of all forms of egotistical pursuit. To eat the bread and drink the cup symbolize a willingness to bring about reconciliation between the nations throughout the world. The local eucharistic celebration is, therefore, the symbol of unity with a worldwide community of believers. Still another level is reconciliation between humans and nature. The Eucharist takes elements from the created universe and transforms them. The bread and the wine are shared in a unique way in the exaltation of Jesus, and they, too, are transformed. To be nourished by the grain of the field and the grape of the vine means to recognize that their place of origin is also sacred. Believers cannot pretend to eat the body of Jesus and drink his blood and yet demonstrate no concern when the earth is raped. The sacramentality of the Eucharist must make believers aware of the sacramentality of the created world.

REVIEW AND/OR DISCUSSION QUESTIONS

1. *What significance does Jesus attach to mutual forgiveness in the Gospels?*

2. *How does reconciliation counteract the hostility in the world perceived by Paul?*

3. *What aspects of reconciliation does Paul emphasize?*

4. *Where is reconciliation most needed in today's world?*

CHAPTER FIVE

Resurrection

INITIAL THOUGHTS

The very term "resurrection" or "rising again" can pose problems. Some people may be tempted to take it literally and thus conceive of resurrection merely as a movement from under the earth to above the earth. By so doing, they fail to see that resurrection is actually a metaphor that focuses on restoration or decisive change.

When "resurrection" or "rising again" is applied to Jesus, it refers to God transforming the person of Jesus. It is not about being brought back to life with the expectation of dying again. Jesus has conquered death. In the final analysis, perhaps the term "transformation" best expresses the image of resurrection.

It is well worth noting that there are two formulations of Jesus' resurrection: (1) he was raised and (2) he rose. According to the first, the Father functions as the agent of the resurrection. This is the earlier of the two expressions and is found, for example, in Paul's first letter "...his Son..., whom he raised from the dead" (1 Thessalonians 1:10). According to the second formulation, Jesus rises by his own power, a formulation that is also found in the same letter. "Jesus died and rose..." (4:14). This expression reflects Jesus' union with the Father (see John 10:30) and his statement that he has power to lay down his life and take it up again (John 10:18).

Sometimes people rather naively state that they are saved solely by the death of Jesus. They thereby exclude the resurrection as an essential component of the whole plan of salvation. For them, Calvary determines everything, while the empty tomb contributes relatively little. In this view, the resurrection functions as the frosting on the cake of Jesus' saving death. However, Paul strenuously opposes this belittling of Jesus' resurrection. In Romans 4:25, he articulates the intrinsic unity of death and resurrection: He "was handed over for our transgressions and was raised for our justification." He spells out the central role of the resurrection when he shows the consequences of denying the resurrection of the body. "If Christ has not been raised, your faith is vain; you are still in your sins" (1 Corinthians 15:17).

BIBLICAL BACKGROUND

Prior to the second century BC, there is no incontestable evidence for the concept of eternal life. However, the metaphor of rising or being raised from the dead suggests at least a hope for somehow overcoming death.

The breakthrough from hope of restoration through resurrection to clear evidence of everlasting life occurs in the Book of Daniel, which was written around 165 BC. Jews who remain loyal to their faith during the persecution of Antiochus IV Epiphanes face martyrdom (see 1 Maccabees 1:54–63). However, the angel offers Daniel this reassuring message: "Many of those who sleep in the dust of the earth shall awake; some to everlasting life, others to reproach and everlasting disgrace" (Daniel 12:2). While this passage in Daniel does not anticipate a universal resurrection or a resurrection of the body, nonetheless God will vindicate his faithful people. Divine justice demands it.

While Daniel does not specify the form of resurrection, 2 Maccabees 7, probably written at the end of the second century BC, views restoration as restoration to an ordinary life, not transformation. In first-century BC Egypt, the author of the Book of Wisdom grounds the foundation of the afterlife in the immortality of the soul, not the resurrection of the body (see 3:1–4). The Jewish world of Palestine into which Jesus was born and the Jewish world of the Diaspora (Jews living outside the Holy Land, including the author of the Book of Wisdom) have no normative belief regarding the afterlife. (During Jesus' ministry, the sect of the Pharisees accepts the resurrection of the body while the sect of the Sadducees flatly denies it.) With Easter Sunday, however, the whole discussion changes. It is Jesus' personal transformation at Easter that holds the promise of resurrection of the body and eternal life for believers.

While Matthew and Mark clearly endorse the resurrection

of Jesus, among the Synoptics, Luke penetrates the theology of Jesus' transformation in his Gospel and the Book of Acts. In his account of the two travelers on the road to Emmaus (Luke 24:13–35), Luke shows that the risen Jesus is the same Jesus, but he has changed. In verse 15, Luke states that the stranger is indeed Jesus himself, but the two disciples fail to recognize him. Jesus then proceeds to unravel the meaning of the Scriptures for them. Significantly, Jesus elaborates on how suffering, death, and resurrection are connected. "Was it not necessary that the Messiah should suffer these things and then enter into his glory" (v. 26)? Eventually Jesus agrees to stay with the travelers (v. 29) and, after being recognized in the breaking of the bread, vanishes (vv. 30–31). For Luke, the risen Jesus is the transformed Jesus who is glorified, but only at the cost of suffering and death.

In Acts, Luke makes two salient points about Jesus' resurrection. The first point is God's capacity to take what is evil and convert it into something good. In a speech in the temple, Peter proclaims, "The author of life you put to death, but God raised him from the dead" (3:15). Similarly, in a speech before the Sanhedrin, Peter once again underlines this process of reversal. "The God of our ancestors raised Jesus, though you had him killed by hanging him on a tree" (5:30). The second point about Jesus' resurrection is that God's action makes him the author of life (3:15) and leader (5:31). The same Greek word that has a slightly different translation in these two passages suggests something like "trailblazer." Hence through his resurrection Jesus has personally opened up the way to eternal life for believers (see also Hebrews 2:10).

In John 11:17–27, the author of the fourth Gospel addresses his community's problem about death, namely if believing in

Jesus means possessing eternal life now (see John 5:24), how do you explain the death of a faithful disciple? In response, Martha, the sister of Lazarus and Mary, represents the community's dilemma. When she confidently declares that her brother will rise on the last day (v. 24), Jesus replies, "I am the resurrection and the life; whoever believes in me, even if he dies, will live, and whoever believes in me, even if he dies, will live" (v. 25). In this profound statement, Jesus personally embodies resurrection and eternal life. In other words, owing to his own transformation experience, he is actually the only way to resurrection and eternal life.

In attempting to solve the problems of his various communities, Paul is compelled to develop the understanding and consequences of Jesus' resurrection. For Paul, the power conferred by the Father envisions not only Jesus, but all humanity, so that they, too, can share in Jesus' experience. In 1 Corinthians 15:20 and 23, Paul speaks of Jesus as the "firstfruits." The image implies that some fruit has already been picked and eventually other fruit will follow. Jesus' resurrection, therefore, announces the general resurrection of all who belong to him.

In Romans 6:1–14, Paul discusses the effects of Christian baptism and its link to Jesus' death and resurrection. In baptism, believers are introduced into Jesus' very act of dying (v. 3). Paul next widens the horizon by including Jesus' burial and resurrection. "We were indeed buried with him through baptism into death, so that just as Christ was raised from the dead by the glory of the Father, we too might live in newness of life" (v. 4). Paul also views the risen Jesus as the actual model or exemplar of the resurrection of believers. "We shall also be united with him in the resurrection" (v. 5).

REFLECTIONS

The notion of Jesus as the first fruits must provide hope for all believers. This image announces that the rest of the crop will be harvested in due time. Jesus' resurrection, therefore, is the harbinger of what is yet to come. With a somewhat similar image, the author of Colossians calls Jesus "the first-born from the dead" (1:18; also see Revelation 1:5). While "firstborn" clearly suggests Jesus' unique position in God's plan, it also looks to other members of his extended family. Jesus thus longs to share his own transformation experience with all his sisters and brothers.

Too often, believers can feel that they are only isolated individuals who lack a sense of destiny. They may conclude that in both life and death they cannot envision any reliable person who will show them the way. Like the author of Hebrews, Luke responds to this dilemma by the image of Jesus as the trailblazer. Like the image of first fruits, trailblazer implies a sense of direction and, as a result, a sense of hope. Considering the abundance of trailblazers in the worlds of science, exploration, sports, etc., believers can reassure themselves that Jesus in and through his resurrection outstrips them all. The light at the end of the tunnel is the light emanating from the empty tomb.

What is there to do when bad things happen to good people? When catastrophe strikes, where can one turn? On several occasions in Acts, Luke reflects on this problem. He does not mask the heinousness of those responsible for the execution of Jesus. However, Luke is not content to recount the event and let it go at that. Rather, he quickly moves on to derive good out of evil. Death cannot be God's final word.

The Living One must respond with new, vibrant life. As Peter expresses it at Pentecost, "God has made him both Lord and Messiah, this Jesus whom you crucified" (2:36). For despairing and discouraged believers, God overcomes evil with good (see Romans 12:21). The resurrection of Jesus does not permit evil to have the last word.

Paul picks up this message of hope when he proclaims that he wants to know the power of Jesus' resurrection (Philippians 3:10). He articulates this hope elsewhere when he teaches his Corinthian converts that Jesus "was crucified out of weakness, but he lives by the power of God" (2 Corinthians 13:4). This resurrection power sustains and energizes him in his arduous ministry. It is this same power that enables believers to move on despite their own personal weaknesses and the difficulties caused by others. The power of Jesus' resurrection makes it possible to see the whole world in a different light.

Paul's thought on the connection between Christian baptism, on the one hand, and the death and resurrection of Jesus, on the other hand, speaks to the concern and hopes of all believers. In Romans 6:3, Paul announces that all the baptized are introduced into Jesus' very own act of dying. However, Paul advances beyond Jesus' death to his resurrection. "Christ was raised from the dead by the glory of the Father..." (v. 4). This intimate sharing in Jesus' death and resurrection must instill a sense of privilege and honor as well as a sense of hope and courage. The experience of Jesus is not a miser's booty—it becomes the patrimony of all believers.

According to John, to accept Jesus as the resurrection and the life is not to dismiss the reality of physical death. Instead, believers are encouraged to see physical death as a moment that leads to the eternal life that Jesus bestows. "Whoever believes in me, even if he dies, will live" (11:25). Jesus himself becomes the model for this transition from death to life. While Jesus totally experiences physical death, that death becomes the stage for birth into glory. "And when I am lifted up from the earth, I will draw everyone to myself" (12:32).

THE EUCHARIST

The Eucharist does not limit itself to the celebration of Jesus' sacrificial death. It advances beyond the shadow of the cross to experience the light emanating from the empty tomb. As the stranger on the road to Emmaus remarks, suffering and death are the condition for the Messiah's entry into glory (see Luke 24:27, 46). By holding both Jesus' death and his resurrection in balance, the Eucharist follows the lead of Acts. "The author of life you put to death, but God raised him from the dead" (3:15). The Jesus whose Body and Blood believers share is the risen Lord who has conquered death.

It is this attitude about the transition from death to eternal life that must engage believers in their celebration of the Eucharist. In the Eucharist, they receive the Jesus who embodies such life. "I am the resurrection and the life" (John 11:25). In the Gospel of John, Jesus assures Martha and believers of all ages that whoever believes in him will never die (11:26). In John's bread of life discourse, Jesus relates this hope of resurrection to the Eucharist. "Whoever eats my flesh and drinks my blood has eternal life, and I will raise him on the last day" (6:54). Other biblical images corroborate Jesus' role as the model or exemplar of the hope of resurrection. He is the first fruits of the resurrection (1 Corinthians 15:20 and 23). He is the firstborn of the dead (Colossians 1:18 and Revelation 1:5). He is the trailblazer leading the way to eternal life (Acts 3:15, 5:31, and Hebrews 2:10). The Eucharist nourishes this hope of resurrection that is patterned on Jesus himself.

For believers, Sunday Eucharist is a celebration of the resurrection. In fact, it has been called a "little Easter." According to the Gospels, Jesus undergoes the transforming experience of resurrection on the first day of the week, Sunday. Luke also mentions the gathering of the Christian community to break bread on the first day of the week (Acts 20:7; also see 1 Corinthians 16:2). Eventually Sunday comes to be called the Lord's Day (Revelation 1:10). Believers, therefore, are invited to see Sunday Eucharist against the background of the resurrection. By receiving the Body and Blood of Jesus each Sunday, they not only recall the resurrection of Jesus but also anticipate their own transformation on the last day. While breaking bread with Jesus and the community on this day reminds them of their journey to heaven, it also empowers them to see the struggles of the week ahead. Sunday Eucharist and the celebration of Jesus' transforming experience sanctify the whole notion of time. Jesus' resurrection, therefore, transcends the limitations of the first century AD and reawakens their hope and confidence with the sanctification of each Sunday. The Risen One at Sunday Eucharist assures believers that he continues to abide with them.

The Eucharist also prepares believers for their own transformation in the resurrection of the body. In his writings, Paul contrasts the resurrected body with the present body. While the present body is perishable, dishonorable, weak, and physical, the resurrected body is imperishable, glorious, powerful, and spiritual. Through baptism, all believers now possess this glory, only in an initial way. However, they will enjoy it completely in their resurrected body. The Eucharist nourishes our bodies for their final encounter with the Lord.

When Paul employs the word "body," he is usually thinking of the whole human person in a concrete human existence. According to Paul, at the general resurrection a person does not merely survive death or is reconfigured as before. Rather, like the Risen One, a person is transformed. The same Spirit that transformed Jesus in his resurrection will also transform believers. Such life beyond death is the complete reintegration of the entire person, a reintegration that believers anticipate in receiving the Body and Blood of the Risen One. The Eucharist and ultimate total transformation share a common bond.

Our professing the mystery of our faith after the consecration situates believers in the time between Jesus' resurrection and his final coming. This in-between time is the time for the celebration of the Eucharist. Encouraged by Jesus' transition from dying to triumph over death by rising again, believers confidently approach the table where Jesus' Body and Blood provide the nourishment to sustain them in their journey. Against the background of Jesus' sacrificial death that culminates in resurrection, the Eucharist is the sacrament that continues to energize believers. As both sacrifice and sacrament, the Eucharist is the abiding symbol of faith, hope, and love.

REVIEW AND/OR DISCUSSION QUESTIONS

1. *What is the difference between "Jesus was raised" and "Jesus rose?"*

2. *What does Paul mean when he describes the risen Jesus as "firstfruits?"*

3. *How does Paul relate Christian baptism to Jesus' death and resurrection?*

4. *How does the Eucharist capture not only Jesus' sacrificial death but also his experience of resurrection?*

CHAPTER SIX

Recognition

INITIAL THOUGHTS

With the exploitation of the computer chip, the world has witnessed an incredible information explosion. Indeed, there appears to be no limit to humanity's exploration and domination of knowledge. On the other hand, an implicit danger may lurk in the relationship between the user and the PC. Such a danger may take place in the manipulation of knowledge to such a degree that knowing is reduced to something that humans manage and control. Admittedly, this is a potential danger, not a proven scenario. While recognizing/knowing can arouse the centripetal urges of ego, it must evoke the desire to share with others. Recognizing/knowing includes community.

Given this context of relationships, one may legitimately pose the question: What does it mean to know another person? Genuine knowledge of another person embraces the entire gamut from vices to virtues, from accomplishments to unexpressed desires, from head to toe. Saying, "I really know you" can be tantamount to saying, "I truly love you."

As will become evident in the prophetic literature, recognizing/knowing God naturally entails obeying and serving God. In acting according to God's will, believers intensify their level of genuine recognition/knowing.

However, believers must also recognize God in others. God is ultimately a God of disguises who chooses to be recognized/known in the painful and disheartening conditions of human life. Although Matthew does not use the verb "to recognize/know" in his account of the final judgment (25:31–46), it is implicit throughout. The criterion of final salvation is to meet the needs of others. By the same token, the criterion of final damnation is to reject the needs of others. In meeting these needs, believers encounter Jesus. In rejecting these needs, believers refuse to encounter Jesus. In feeding the hungry, giving drink to the thirsty, etc., the first group will hear these words from Jesus, "Amen, I say to you, whatever you did for one of these least brothers of mine, you did for me" (v. 40).

BIBLICAL BACKGROUND

In the Old Testament, recognizing/knowing is more a personal encounter than an impersonal declaration of objective facts. For example, in depicting the renewed marriage relationship between the Lord and Israel, Hosea announces, "I will betroth you to me forever...and you shall know the LORD" (2:21–22). Then the prophet parallels steadfast love with knowledge of God, indicating that Israel must recognize God in loyalty and fidelity. To not recognize/know is to violate the intimate covenantal relationship between the Lord and Israel. In accusing Israel of lacking knowledge of God, Hosea subsequently enumerates the specific sins that this disloyalty entails, namely swearing, lying, murder, stealing, and adultery (4:1–2). According to Jeremiah, this personal recognition of the rights of the sovereign is what is lacking in Israel's relationship with the Lord. "They go from evil to evil, and me they do not know—oracle of the LORD" (9:2).

The prophet Ezekiel seems to be obsessed with knowledge. More than seventy times he uses the "recognition formula" that consists of two components: (1) "and you (they) shall know" and (2) an object, namely "that I am the Lord." Basically, this formula is a self-introduction that reveals an unnamed someone who now abandons that anonymous posture by sharing his personal name. Ezekiel follows a certain order in this process: (1) a description of God's actions and (2) the act of human recognition. For example, in Ezekiel 7:2–4, the prophet announces (vv. 2–4a) the destruction of the land of Israel because of human sinfulness and concludes with, "then you shall you know that I am the LORD" (v. 4b). Thus, God's actions against his people are calculated to lead them to recognition. This recognition is nothing less than the awareness or acknowledgment that God cannot and will not tolerate such sinful behavior.

Ezekiel also uses this recognition formula when he delivers oracles of hope and reconstruction in the aftermath of exilic despair and frustration. In the vision of the dry bones

(37:1–14), the prophet proclaims amid this catastrophe that God will intervene and restore them to the land of Israel. When they come to life again owing to God's spirit, they will "know that I am the LORD" (v. 6). When God opens their graves and brings them up from them, they will "know that I am the LORD" (v. 13).

The Gospel of Mark develops this theme of recognition/ knowledge in a negative way, especially in the description of the Twelve. First, they do not recognize who Jesus is. After the first miracle of the loaves, they still do not perceive who Jesus is because of their hardness of heart (6:52). Second, they reject Jesus' strategy of suffering. This provokes Jesus to label Peter a Satan (8:33) and upbraid the Twelve as a whole for being devotees of power and prestige (9:32 and 10:35–45). Third, they abandon Jesus in the garden and take to flight (14:50). Fourth, Peter denies Jesus three times, going so far as to take this oath: "I do not know this man about whom you are talking" (14:71). Although the Twelve do not really recognize who Jesus is, Mark ends his Gospel with the account of the resurrection and the promise of forgiveness in a renewed relationship. Despite their disloyalty, Jesus breaks the vicious cycle of human malice with the gift of reconciliation. The Gospel readers and hearers are encouraged to believe that they, too, will come to know Jesus and recognize him in their own sufferings and remorse.

In the Gospel and Letters of John, recognizing/knowing plays a pivotal role. It includes the focus on Jesus' mission (John 17:3), the relationship between Jesus and his Father (John 7:29 and 8:55), and the bond between Jesus and his disciples (John 10:14–15). After the manner of the prophetic tradition, the one who knows God keeps his commandments

(1 John 2:3–5). For John, the believer who knows Jesus, in turn knows the Father (John 14:7) since "the Father is in me and I am in the Father" (10:38). Since Jesus' opponents reject him, they demonstrate (1) that they do not know the Father and (2) that they do not know him (8:19).

The Gospel of John also teaches that the process of getting to recognize/know Jesus is a gradual one. In the account of the Samaritan woman (4:5–42), she first identifies Jesus as a Jew (v. 9), then calls him "sir" (v. 11), and then asks whether he is greater than her ancestor, Jacob (v. 12). As the conversation continues, she concludes that Jesus must be a prophet (v. 19) and proceeds to speak about the Messiah. She then asks her townspeople whether he is the Messiah (v. 29). Because of her testimony, many of the townspeople come to believe in him (v. 39). In turn, they inform the woman that they accept Jesus as Savior of the world because of their own encounter with him (v. 41). In the account of the healing of the man born blind (9:1–41), the same gradual process of recognizing/knowing Jesus is operative. He initially labels Jesus a man, but then calls him a prophet (v. 17) and attests that he comes from God (v. 33). Finally, he accepts Jesus as the Son of Man and worships him (v. 38).

In 1 Corinthians 8, some members of that community make an exclusive claim to having knowledge (v. 1). In reply, Paul remarks that knowledge is not the prerogative of any one group. He adds that one must distinguish knowledge from love. He further observes that the know-it-alls in Corinth do not have the right kind of knowledge. Finally, he insists, "if one loves God, one is known by him" (v. 3). For Paul, knowledge of God presumes an experience of God in which there is a reciprocal exchange of knowledge on the part of God and the believer. To be known by God is, in effect, to be recognized or acknowledged by God. Here Paul handles the question of knowledge by raising it to the level of being known rather than knowing.

Paul picks up this theme in 1 Corinthians 13, where he contrasts the present (seeing in a mirror) with the end time (face to face). "At present, I know partially; then I shall know fully, as I am fully known" (v. 12). Paul, therefore, compares this future knowledge with the reality of having been known by God before the creation of the world. To be known by God is to have an experience of God that he himself initiates.

In Philippians 3, Paul pursues once again the rich theme of recognizing/knowing God in Christ. He writes: "More than that, I even consider everything as loss because of the supreme good of knowing Christ Jesus my Lord" (v. 8). Therefore, to have a deep personal relationship with Jesus outstrips everything else. A few verses later Paul adds that he yearns "to know Christ and the power of his resurrection" (v. 10). For Paul, to know Christ is to experience him in the transforming power of his resurrection whereby he becomes a life-giving spirit (see 1 Corinthians 15:45). Hence, recognizing/knowing Christ is intimately bound up with the overwhelming force of his resurrection.

REFLECTIONS

Against this rich biblical background, recognizing/knowing God and being recognized/known by him are anything but a dull, cerebral encounter. From the biblical perspective, one must underline the deep personal nature of this experience. In the final analysis, recognition/knowledge involves a process of sharing where the believer gains access to and intimacy with

God. To that extent, God cannot be an anonymous being who remains aloof. Recognizing/knowing God does more than enrich human life. It raises life to a completely new level where God is not the celestial administrator computing human pluses and minuses, but the divine lover who shares closeness and warmth in the act of recognizing/knowing.

The accounts of the Samaritan woman and the man born blind powerfully remind believers that recognizing/knowing is indeed a gradual process. Here the human experience of recognizing/knowing serves as a good analogy. People usually do not recognize/know another person immediately. Rather, through time and effort they begin to perceive the character and depth of another. It is not necessarily a matter of divulging secrets but of listening to and searching for what constitutes another. To recognize/know God now is to see in a mirror dimly. However, to recognize/know God in the end time is to see face-to-face (1 Corinthians 13:12).

The prophetic insistence on recognizing/knowing God through loyalty and fidelity possesses immense value for all believers. Obedient response to God's will becomes the criterion for measuring true recognition/knowledge. One recognizes/knows in proportion to one's submission to the will of God. Commandments are not impersonal limitations on human liberty. Rather, they become highly personal expressions of recognizing/knowing God. It is not by accident that the prophet Hosea parallels steadfast love with knowledge of God (6:6).

Ezekiel's recognition formula must rouse believers to assess the events of daily life, whether they are positive or negative. When insatiable desire for pleasure and dehumanizing domination of others lead to pain and disaster, believers must recognize/know in these events "that I am the LORD." When the unflagging practice of social justice and the unstinting generosity of self-giving to others result in the restoration of the marginalized and the reinstatement of truly human values, believers must then recognize/know "that I am the LORD." To recognize/know God in human history is to recognize/ know the one who broke into that history by becoming flesh (John 1:14).

Matthew's theology of disguises (25:31–46) must urge believers to recognize/know God in others, particularly those who are suffering. To discover God in these hungry, thirsty, naked people is to recognize/know God, who adopts a variety of masks and scenarios to prompt genuine human response. In other words, to alleviate the pain and anguish of such people is to practice the fine art of recognizing/knowing God. Those truly bent on such a fine art must dare to look beyond the exterior to capture the divine image in the interior. To recognize/know and resolve the anguish of such people is to recognize/know the one who "was crucified out of weakness, but he lives by the power of God" (2 Corinthians 13:4).

THE EUCHARIST

Luke's account of the travelers on the road to Emmaus (24:13–35) focuses, among other things, on: (1) the celebration of the Eucharist (the breaking of the bread) and (2) the recognition of Jesus in this very act. In initially declining the travelers' invitation to stay with them, Jesus eventually accepts and joins them for a meal. "While he was with them at table, he took bread, said the blessing, broke it, and gave it to them. With that their eyes were opened and they recognized him" (vv. 30–31; also see v. 35). Here the two disciples who represent all the others who choose to walk away from God's plan of glory via suffering and death (vv. 19–21) recognize Jesus, who refuses to walk away from them. He makes himself known to them and reroutes them back to Jerusalem. In the breaking of the bread, he shares his transformed life with them. The outcome is that they thereby come to recognize him.

Believers can readily identify with the two travelers and their problems. Good Friday had dashed all their hopes—everything seemed all too useless so that "cut and run" became the only viable alternative. Christians today also face a myriad of concerns and worries. Their sense of loneliness can become so acute that their faith can become endangered. They, too, want to continue walking away from their Jerusalem. Given this lamentable situation, they can learn from the two travelers. As Jesus explained the Scriptures concerning his destiny, their hearts were burning within them (v. 32). Nonetheless, "their eyes were prevented from recognizing him" (v. 16). It was only in the breaking of the bread that the scales fell from their eyes and "they recognized him" (v. 31). For today's travelers who are also burdened with a multitude of worries, Jesus in the Eucharist provides the solution. His presence in the breaking of the bread assures them that they are not alone, that he continues to journey with them, and that their problems are not insurmountable. Recognition of Jesus in the Eucharist turns their lives around in the direction of Jerusalem.

In Acts 2:42, Luke describes key characteristics of the early Christian community in Jerusalem: "the teaching of the apostles and to the communal life, to the breaking of the bread and to the prayers." The breaking of the bread is Luke's expression, as in Luke 24:35, for the Eucharist (see Acts 2:46). Luke sees the breaking of the bread as the source of life for the Christian community (Acts 20:7–12) and the means of salvation (27:33–36). In all of these instances, Jesus is present, responding to the needs of those in attendance, whether for food, healing, or instruction. To break bread is to recognize Jesus as still present in their midst.

Believers today recognize Jesus in their breaking of the bread with him. As in Acts, he provides food, healing, and instruction. In this act of recognition, they realize that Jesus never ceases to be present. Like the Emmaus travelers, they gather hope and courage to resume their journey. Recognition of Jesus in the Eucharist, however, must lead to recognition of Jesus in others. His extended family often suffers from want of food, from sickness, and from faulty teaching. Believers are challenged to recognize such needs and address them. In this way, the recognition of Jesus in the breaking of the bread sustains and strengthens them for breaking open the message of hope in the lives of others.

Believers are called upon not only to recognize Jesus in the Eucharist and in the concerns of others, but also to make themselves recognizable as Christians. Instead of carrying the eucharistic Lord in public through the city streets, believers are challenged to make themselves recognizable as followers of the Lord by the caliber of their lives. The Eucharist provides both the courage and the nourishment to carry out this demanding ministry. The Eucharist sustains them as they show a weary world that Jesus is still in their midst. This is indeed another form of "true presence."

REVIEW AND/OR DISCUSSION QUESTIONS

1. *How do the prophets understand the expression "to know God?"*

2. *How does the prophet Ezekiel employ the recognition formula in his ministry?*

3. *How does Mark develop the theme of the Twelve not recognizing who Jesus really is?*

4. *What do the accounts of the Samaritan woman and the man born blind in the Gospel of John say about the process of recognizing/knowing Jesus?*

CHAPTER SEVEN

Remembrance

INITIAL THOUGHTS

When people hear the verb "to remember," they often translate it automatically as "not to forget." Frequently they conjure up the function of memory as providing a storehouse of facts and figures that one forgets only at one's peril. At the same time, they may see memory as solely static, computer-like recall. They also realize the fragility of memory, a fragility captured in the expression, "I'll never forget what's-his-name."

Most people will balk when someone remarks that memory is linked to destiny. Since memory is simply the impersonal retrieval of past information, these people cannot possibly imagine that memory constitutes identity. Thus, they blatantly reject the axiom, "We become what we remember." However, the process of selecting and choosing persons and objects to remember reveals the makeup of people. What they preserve in their memory bank indicates their code of ethics, their prejudices, their unexpressed feelings, etc. Memory, therefore, functions as a type of ID that exposes the real me. People indeed become what they remember.

The American philosopher George Santayana coined the famous saying that "those who do not remember the past are condemned to repeat it." Memory is then linked to history. The danger now becomes one of selective memory. One is thus tempted to banish from memory all atrocities, such as ethnic cleansing. The challenge, however, is to overcome such selectivity by daring to recall both the triumph of victory and the agony of defeat. The past continues to stand both as a challenge and a beacon of hope.

Usually, remembering is relegated to the past. It has to do with recalling persons from the past and events that took place a while ago. Ironically, however, remembering also has a future function. The recall of persons and events in the past impinges on human conduct in the future. Remembering what occurred with particular people in the past forms a plan of action for the future, for better or worse. To that extent, remembering can become an activity fraught with danger since the material stored in memory can function either constructively or destructively. Memory, therefore, embraces past, present, and future.

Usually, people envision remembering as a purely human activity. They dare not attribute that function to God, since the deity is all-knowing and invincible. The Bible, however, suggests otherwise. Especially in the Old Testament, God is remembered for remembering. In such instances, God's recall and believers' pleas for divine assistance illustrate God's involvement in human affairs, frequently desperate situations. In the art of remembering, God does not merely extract past information. Rather, God recalls his commitment to the covenant and, therefore, his obligation to serve his covenant partners. In remembering, God serves as his people's guarantor and protector.

BIBLICAL BACKGROUND

The Old Testament features remembering on the part of both God and humans. With regard to the former, God takes his covenant partners with all seriousness and, in remembering, forges an identity. God then remains faithful to this identity and acts according to it. For example, God remembers Noah when the time comes to stop the flood (Genesis 8:1). He remembers Abraham and so delivers his nephew, Lot, when he overthrows Sodom and Gomorrah (19:29). God remembers Rachel when he enables her to conceive (30:22). He also remembers the plight of the Israelites in Egypt and promises to deliver them from bondage (Exodus 2:24 and 6:5–6).

On several occasions, Israel pleads with God to remember. Samson asks God to remember by strengthening him to take revenge on the Philistines (Judges 16:28). The barren Hannah begs God to give her a baby boy: "O LORD of hosts, if you look with pity on the hardship of your servant, if you remember me and do not forget me..." (1 Samuel 1:11). During a great drought the people of Judah beseech God not to despise them but remember them by sending rain (Jeremiah

14:22). At a time of great despair and anguish, the prophet Jeremiah challenges God's memory, saying, "remember me and take care of me, avenge me on my persecutors" (15:15). In all these instances of remembering, God establishes his identity by covenantal fidelity, especially on behalf of the distraught.

Such divine remembering becomes a basis for praise of God in the Book of Psalms. In Psalm 105:8, the psalmist prefaces his long recital of God's interventions in Israel's history with the observation that God is forever mindful of his covenant. Genuine religious fervor reveals itself in Israel's beseeching God to remember. Such petitions lead God to bless. "The LORD remembers us and will bless us" (115:12).

God's people also exercise the ministry of remembering. Moses exhorts the people to remember the Exodus (Exodus 13:3). Such remembering will provide a sense of community and continuity. The feast of Unleavened Bread is to serve as a memorial of God's deliverance from Egypt (12:14). In Deuteronomy, the people of Israel face no greater temptation than forgetting through disobedience. "Be careful to not forget the LORD, your God, by failing to keep his commandments" (8:11). According to Deuteronomy 5:15, the motive provided for observing the Sabbath is remembrance of the Exodus. This remembrance links continuity with the past to fidelity in new situations. In depicting the reconstructed city of Jerusalem, Isaiah presents the city sentinels as actually reminding the Lord incessantly about the city's needs and divine obligation (Isaiah 62:6). For the prophet, the Lord needs reminding, lest he forget.

There are fewer instances of remembering on the part of God in the New Testament. However, Mary's Magnificat and Zechariah's Benedictus emphasize that God has remembered to fulfill the promises made to Israel's ancestors. In the Benedictus, Zechariah prays "to show mercy to our fathers, and to be mindful of his holy covenant" (Luke 1:72; also see 1:54). In Acts, an angel informs Cornelius that his prayers and almsgiving remind God to act favorably on his behalf (10:4, 31). In the vision of the fall of Babylon (Rome) the seer of Revelation hears a heavenly voice confirming that God has remembered her iniquities and will take proper action (18:5; also see 16:19). No doubt the most famous petition to remember in the New Testament comes from the lips of the so-called good thief (Luke 23:42). His request that Jesus remember him upon coming into his kingdom echoes Joseph's request to the chief cupbearer to remember him upon his reinstatement by Pharaoh (Genesis 40:14).

Remembering on the part of humans is not lacking in the New Testament. Jesus assures his audience at Bethany that the good deed performed by the anonymous anointing woman "will be told in memory of her" (Mark 14:9). After denying Jesus for the third time, Peter hears the cock crowing and remembers Jesus' prediction (Mark 14:72). Paul praises his Corinthian community "because you remember me in everything and hold fast to the traditions, just as I handed them on to you" (1 Corinthians 11:2; also see 4:17). In these three instances, remembering involves much more than static recall. Remembering establishes the identity of the anointing woman, Peter, and the Corinthian Christians.

Authentic remembering plays a conspicuous role after the resurrection. At the empty tomb, two men instruct the anointing women that they can understand Jesus' resurrection by remembering what he told them about his death and subsequent exoneration (Luke 24:7–8). When Jesus says that he will raise up the temple in three days, the disciples do not understand. However, after his resurrection, they remember his saying and realize that Jesus was referring to the temple of his body (John 2:19–22). On Palm Sunday, Jesus enters Jerusalem in triumph on a donkey, "'your king comes, seated upon an ass's colt!' His disciples did not understand this at first; but when Jesus had been glorified they remembered" (12:15–16). At the Last Supper, Jesus assures his disciples that the Spirit, the Paraclete, will bring to mind everything that he told them (14:26).

There is an interesting parallel between Israel's obligation to remember the Exodus and the Church's imperative to recall Jesus' resurrection. In freeing a male slave, the Israelite must treat him generously. "Remember that you too were slaves in the land of Egypt, and the LORD, your God, redeemed you" (Deuteronomy 15:15). In his letter, the author of 2 Timothy implicitly seeks to alert the recipient that pain and suffering precede exaltation. He then commands, "Remember Jesus Christ, raised from the dead" (2:8). Loyalty, in both cases, hinges on obedient remembrance of God's decisive actions, namely the Exodus and the resurrection. To recall these saving events is to find identity through fidelity.

REFLECTIONS

When the Old Testament highlights God's involvement in the Exodus and the New Testament emphasizes God's intervention in the resurrection, believers may reasonably add a personal motive to their remembering God. The motive is nothing less than God's call to faith. Recalling their baptism does not diminish the importance or centrality of the Exodus and resurrection. Rather, it locates their baptism in a series of actions whereby God enters human history and reorients it. It is during the Easter season that believers can especially exercise this ministry of remembering. Such remembering reinforces their identity in Christ and their call to service. Memory, identity, and involvement are intimately connected.

Believers must also function after the manner of Jerusalem's sentinels in Isaiah 62:6. They must constantly remind God of their needs. They must bring to his attention their pressing hurts and problems. Prayer thus becomes one aspect of the ministry of memory. Believers must not hesitate to badger God. In continuity with the psalmist, they must make this demand, "Awake! Why do you sleep, O LORD? Rise up! Do not reject us forever" (Psalm 44:24)! Such prayer serves to remind God that he has pledged his covenant word of steadfast love. Prayer thus prods God to remember.

In this connection, the *Memorare* (literally, "remember"), a traditional prayer to Mary, the mother of Jesus, may function as a model for the type of prayer outlined above. The prayer begins with the mention of Mary's history of responding to the needs of her devotees ("that never was it known that anyone who fled to thy protection, implored thy help...was left unaided"). Inspired by Mary's track record, the petitioner seeks her mediation and addresses her as "Mother of the Word Incarnate." The prayer concludes with the request for Mary's intercession. Remembering the history of Marian intervention serves as a powerful incentive for present needs. Prayer to Mary situates believers not only in the context of her Son but also under the umbrella of Israel's ancestors. In her Magnificat, she prays, "He has helped Israel his servant, remembering his mercy, according to his promise to our fathers, to Abraham and to his descendants forever" (Luke 1:54–55).

According to the Gospel of John, the Paraclete, the Spirit, assists believers in the ministry of memory. "The holy Spirit... will teach you everything, and remind you of all that [I] told you" (14:26). As noted earlier, the task of reminding is not reducible to sterile recalling. The Paraclete does not revive the forgotten. Rather, he moves believers to penetrate the depth and richness of Jesus' message. Reminding thereby becomes a process whereby believers can initiate actions based on Jesus' teaching. Through the Paraclete's act of reminding, believers can perceive Jesus' message in a new light.

THE EUCHARIST

Unlike Matthew and Mark, Luke has Jesus declare, "Do this in memory of me" (22:19), after identifying the bread as Jesus' body. In this context, remembering plays a vital role, since Luke has constructed the Last Supper scene (22:14–38) as a farewell speech. Following the lead of Jacob's speech in Genesis 47—50 and Joshua's speech in Joshua 23—24, Luke depicts Jesus against the background of his impending death. As a literary genre, this farewell speech, however, underscores not so much the fate of the speaker as the future of those addressed. Thus, Luke has Jesus predict attacks on his disciples (Luke 22:31–34) and recommends the ideal form of behavior (vv. 24–27).

Far from being a static recall of past events, this remembrance at the Last Supper takes the disciples beyond Jesus' death to the period of the post-Easter Church. By their remembrance, the disciples form a link between the past and the future. Luke

composes his second volume, the Acts of the Apostles, to connect the mission of Jesus with the mission of the Church. To
reach this goal, Luke situates the need for repentance against
the backdrop of recall of God's past acts of deliverance with
emphasis on Jesus' own mission to Israel. For example, in the
Cornelius scene, Peter recalls the ministry of Jesus that culmi-
nated in his death and resurrection that now impacts the recep-
tion of gentiles into the Christian community (Acts 10:34–48).
Similarly at Pisidian Antioch Paul reminds his audience of the
Exodus, as well as the roles of Samuel, Saul, and David, only
to focus on the mission of Jesus. "What God promised our
ancestors he has brought to fulfillment for us, [their] children,
by raising up Jesus" (Acts 13:32–33).

In celebrating the Eucharist, today's believers hear once
again the command to remember. They are not urged to recite
chapter and verse concerning the events of Holy Week. Rather,
like the disciples in Luke-Acts, they are exhorted to forge that
vital link between the past and the present by remembering
the mission of Jesus in their own time and setting. By doing
so, they are more than storytellers rehearsing scenes from the
past. Instead, they function as witnesses who value the legacy
of the past for the needs of the present moment. In offering
hope, in consoling, in instructing, etc., they recall that Jesus'
death-resurrection touches them even now. To remember,
especially through decisive action, is to rejoin the disciples at
the Last Supper and participate in their ministry. Simply put,
that ministry is to keep the memory of Jesus alive, infectious,
and contagious here and now.

Like Luke, Paul also introduces the remembrance command
in quoting the words of institution. However, unlike Luke,
Paul does so after both the bread and the cup: "Do this, as

often as you drink it, in remembrance of me" (1 Corinthians 11:25). In view of the divisiveness of the Corinthian community, especially as seen in their eucharistic celebrations, Paul's insistence on remembrance is telling. As Paul sees it, the Corinthians remember Jesus only in terms of the past. For him, however, authentic memory embraces the present as well as the future. In recalling Jesus' total self-giving on Calvary, Christians are to act upon it in the present and the future. The dying of Jesus must become so fixed in their minds that it prompts them to act accordingly, both in the present and in the future. If the Corinthians truly remembered the dying of Jesus, they would not get involved in rivalries and factions. True recall of the past becomes the criterion for action in the present and the future.

Modern believers should not dismiss Paul's scolding of the Corinthians as simply old, to-be-forgotten history. They too easily face the same dilemma by limiting memory merely to the past. In their celebration of the Eucharist, the self-giving of Jesus in death should be so uppermost in their memory that it compels them to act according to that model. In their fidelity to their Christian calling, in their commitment to others, in their reaching out to the unfortunate, they refine the delicate art of remembering. To break bread with Jesus must remind them to recall and address the concerns of his extended family.

REVIEW AND/OR DISCUSSION QUESTIONS

1. *According to the Old Testament, in what types of situations does God usually remember?*

2. *According to the Old Testament, how do the Israelites move God to remember?*

3. *How does memory function in the Gospel of John in the aftermath of Jesus' resurrection?*

4. *In his formula for the institution of the Eucharist, why does Paul mention the command to remember twice (1 Corinthians 11:24–25)?*

CHAPTER EIGHT

Re-creation

INITIAL THOUGHTS

This notion of creation as an ongoing reality may strike some as rather strange. However, the biblical authors take re-creation as yet another indication of God's involvement with humanity. God continues to create by intervening in human history and interacting with his creatures, the work of his hands. Ongoing creation demonstrates God's abiding concern for all his creation. Through ongoing creation, God refuses to limit his capacity to provide surprises for his creatures. To continue to create is to articulate God's refusal to accept a static, nonrenewable world.

The rite of baptism provides an instructive example of re-creation. Baptism is a new birth, a newness that the baptismal garment symbolizes since the baptized have indeed clothed themselves in Christ and thus constitute a new creation. By embracing the newness of the resurrection, they are personally involved in God's action of ongoing creation. The empty tomb has filled them with an indescribable dimension of new life.

The role of the Spirit cannot be underestimated. God, who breathed on the waters and turned chaos into cosmos, continues to breathe, suffusing life and vitality of limitless proportions. Owing to the role of the Spirit, the baptized experience God's life on a new level. As in Ezekiel's vision of the dry bones, "the breath entered them; they came to life and stood on their feet..." (37:10). With the Spirit comes the newness of ongoing creation. The words of Psalm 104:30 seem totally appropriate: "Send forth your spirit, they are created and you renew the face of the earth."

With new creation come new responsibilities. Through baptism, believers enter into a new relationship with God and their community. They assume the obligation of translating their new creation into action through fidelity and obedience. Fresh from the hand of the Creator, they are to breathe new life into those segments of their world where the eroding power of sin has left only death and grief. They are to overcome darkness by being light for the world. They are to defeat despair by being hope for their world. Expressed in another way, they are to bring their baptismal garment unstained to Jesus' judgment seat.

BIBLICAL BACKGROUND

In the first creation account (Genesis 1:1—2:4a), one must note that the author does not intend to narrate in a scientific way how the world and humankind actually came into being. As a matter of fact, he faces a more crucial task, namely to provide a message of hope. Probably envisioning the seemingly hopeless situation of the Jewish exiles in Babylon (sixth century BC), he paints a challenging picture of God overcoming the chaos of their lives. Using a six-day schema, he assigns works of separation (for example, light from darkness) to days one through four, and works of adornment (for example, the sun and the moon) to days four through six. On the sixth day, God reaches the high point of his creative energy with the creation of the human couple. The author concludes with God's rest on the seventh day. The entire account is one of hope for the beleaguered audience. Chaos can give way to cosmos through God's act of creating.

How should humans respond to ongoing creation? Psalm 8 addresses this issue by posing the dilemma of such re-creation. "What is man that you are mindful of him, and a son of man that you care for him" (v. 5)? The psalmist contrasts babes and infants with foes, the enemy, and the avenger (v. 3). Will humans react like little children who naturally blurt out their praise of the Creator, or will they respond as God's opponents by refusing to accept the limitations of being human? While God has raised humans to the level of royalty (v. 6, "crowned him with glory and honor"), they must respect this status by fidelity to their Creator, not opposition.

Psalm 104, a hymn or psalm of descriptive praise like Psalm 8, speaks of God's work of creation in verses 2–4 by using participles in the Hebrew text that indicate ongoing activity. Fundamentally, this exquisite poem sings of the symmetry and splendor of God's re-creation. At the same time, it accentuates the connectedness of all creation. All depend on God's providence and care. "All of these look to you to give them food in due time" (v. 27). The psalm also underlines the role of humans in re-creation. "People go out to their work, to their labor until evening falls" (v. 23). Far from being drudgery, human effort is intended to be another form of praise of the Creator.

The prophet Isaiah proclaims a message of newness in God's ongoing creation. In expressing this word of hope to his frustrated exiles, he announces that God will do the unexpected. "Remember not the events of the past, the things of long ago consider not" (43:18–19). God, who will break through their crushing despair, is the one who created in the beginning. "But now, thus says the LORD, who created you, Jacob, and formed you, Israel: Do not fear, for I have redeemed you" (43:1). God, who overcame chaos in the first creation, will now defeat the hopelessness of his people by establishing a new Exodus in which they will cross the desert from Babylon to Jerusalem (40:3–5). With the miracle of ongoing creation, the people must break out with appropriate music. "Sing to the LORD a new song, his praise from the ends of the earth" (42:10).

In place of the gutted and languishing capital, the New Jerusalem will be the handiwork of this cosmic sovereign. The city will be a joy and its people a delight (65:18). This work of divine reconstruction will not tolerate any sound of weeping or cry of distress (v. 19). The building of new houses and the planting of new vineyards (vv. 21–22) will signal the fulfillment of the Creator's promise. All that was sordid and defiled in the past will be clean and pure in the ancient but new city. Boundless joy is the only proper response. "Be glad forever in what I am creating" (v. 18).

The baptism of Jesus clearly marks a watershed in his life as he leaves his family and occupation in Nazareth to assume his ministry. His baptism echoes God's creative work in the beginning: water, Spirit, and bird (dove). "On coming up out of the water he saw the heavens being torn open and the Spirit, like a dove, descending upon him" (Mark 1:10). In Genesis 1:2, a mighty wind/breath/spirit hovers over the waters. The hovering suggests the motion of a bird as in Deuteronomy 32:11: "As an eagle...hovering over its young." For Mark's audience the baptism of Jesus reveals that the end time (Jesus' mission, etc.) is a new beginning. Jesus at his baptism is interpreted against the backdrop of ongoing creation.

The rite of baptism and the putting on of new clothes receive great attention in Paul's Letter to the Galatians. "For all of you who were baptized into Christ have clothed yourselves with Christ" (3:27). Paul may be alluding to the practice whereby baptismal candidates remove their clothes, are baptized, and put on new clothes after coming out of the baptismal waters. By putting on Christ, the newly baptized are incorporated into Christ. Paul is implying that baptism causes a radical transformation whereby the candidates relinquish their old identity and get a new one, namely in Christ. The newly baptized, the recipients of God's ongoing creation, are thereby empowered to lead a new life in Christ.

In this same letter, Paul strenuously opposes the efforts of those who seek to impose Judaism on his pagan converts in Galatia by insisting, for example, on the need for circumcision and the observance of Jewish food laws. The cross completely separates Paul from the previously known entire religious world, that is, both Jewish (circumcision) and pagan (uncircumcision). Hence he writes, "For neither does circumcision mean anything, nor does uncircumcision, but only a new creation" (6:15). A new creation, therefore, has replaced the old world, not merely repaired it. God has accomplished this new creation through the cross of Jesus (6:14). The Church is incorporated into Christ, the new creation. The Israel of God embodies this new creation by mutual service to the people whom God calls into existence, not in the Jewish Law, but in Christ.

In 2 Corinthians, Paul, who judged Jesus falsely while a Pharisee, takes up the issue of believers judging other human beings. He writes, "So whoever is in Christ is a new creation: the old things have passed away; behold, new things have come" (5:17). God's work in Christ is pictured as ongoing creation so that believers are indeed constituted a new creation. For Paul, the transformation is so radical that everything old has vanished and everything new has become the proper focus of attention. Perhaps Paul is here recalling Isaiah's admonition, "Remember not the events of the past, the things of long ago consider not; See I am doing something new" (43:18–19)!

In Romans, Paul reflects on the relationship between humans and creation. Because of the enslaving power of human sin, creation has also suffered enslavement. However, "creation itself would be set free from slavery to corruption and share in the glorious freedom of the children of God" (8:21). Because of the close bond between creation and humanity, creation is experiencing labor pains in its passage from slavery to freedom (8:22). While humans also participate in creation's pains, they enjoy a hope based on possession of the Spirit (8:23). Just as the Spirit is the transforming agent in Jesus' resurrection, that same Spirit is the transforming agent in the re-creation of the material universe. Jesus, humans, and the material world are inexorably interconnected.

The Gospel of John also emphasizes ongoing creation in his accounts of Jesus' death and resurrection. The mention of a garden in the narratives of Jesus' arrest (18:1) and his burial (19:41) and Mary Magdalene's identification of Jesus as a gardener (20:15) recall the Garden of Eden story. The notion of incompletion and completion of work provides additional reference to Genesis 2:2–3, where God rests on the seventh day after completing the work of creation. In John 5:17, Jesus states that his Father and he are still working (see also 4:34 and 5:36). However, on the cross Jesus realizes that all is now finished and, after receiving the wine, announces, "It is finished" (19:30). Through his death, Jesus brings the work his Father began in the first creation to completion. Finally, the indications of time also establish a connection with the first creation. According to 20:1 and 19, Jesus' resurrection takes place on "the first day of the week," a phrase that links Jesus' resurrection to God's creative work in the beginning. Moreover, the phrase "a week later" in 20:26, when the risen Jesus appears to the disciples a second time with Thomas present, suggests the first day of a new week when Jesus renews creation. Briefly put, the resurrection of Jesus has inaugurated a new creation.

REFLECTIONS

The newness experienced by believers is grounded in the transformation achieved by Jesus in his resurrection. Baptized into Christ, they have clothed themselves in Christ (Galatians 3:27). This image of clothing is not something purely external. Rather, it involves a profound change in the very makeup of the person. Having entered into Jesus' experience, they are intimately united with him. In the expression of Second Corinthians 5:17, the person in Christ is a new creation—the old has given way to the new. In turn, this means that the prism for judging others is the freshness of God's ongoing creation in Christ.

Closely linked to this divine act of ongoing creation is the role of the Spirit. At the initial creation, the Spirit hovers over the waters, commencing the movement from chaos to cosmos. At the baptism of Jesus, the Spirit empowers him to begin to exercise his ministry. With the baptism of believers comes the challenge to breathe the Spirit on others. They become God's agents for hovering over the unruly waters of chaos in their world. Their baptism, therefore, energizes them to undertake this demanding ministry. They are the channels of God's grace, equipped to promote love instead of hate, and concern instead of apathy. To breathe forth the Spirit is to foster re-creation.

Believers are also bound up with the transformation of the material world. They must demonstrate respect for the created world, a respect that derives from the presence of the Creator and the responsibility inherent in the human task to provide for a more human world. Ecology and re-creation go hand in hand.

Having become a new creation, believers must proclaim a message of all-consuming hope. In this respect, they are not unlike Isaiah. He encountered the despair and hopelessness of his fellow exiles. Undaunted by this harrowing situation, he announced a new Exodus, this time from Babylon, not Egypt. "In the wilderness prepare the way of the LORD! Make straight in the wasteland a highway for our God" (40:3)! He preached a message of newness to dispel timidity and fear. Believers carry the torch of this singular prophet by communicating hope through word and deed. They must encourage their generation to dare to hope, a commodity too often in short supply. They must assure their audience of the insuperable love of God. "Do not fear, for I have redeemed you; I have called you by name: you are mine" (Isaiah 43:1). The defeat of despair is but another instance of ongoing creation.

THE EUCHARIST

Ongoing creation and the Eucharist share much in common. In the creation account of Genesis 1 the spirit/wind/breath of God hovers over the unruly waters of chaos. God's word then initiates the process whereby chaos gives way to cosmos. At the baptism of Jesus, the Spirit in the form of a dove energizes Jesus as he emerges from the water to begin his ministry. The end time (the start of his ministry) is like the beginning in Genesis 1. On Easter morning, at the command of the Father, the Spirit comes upon the dead body of Jesus and transforms him into a life-giving spirit (1 Corinthians 15:45). Similarly, at the celebration of the Eucharist the presider calls upon the Father to let the Spirit come upon the gifts of bread and wine so that they may become the Body and Blood of the Son. The Eucharist is but another instance of re-creation.

Believers are urged not to be silent bystanders at this celebration, but to become involved participants in their world of ongoing creation. In effect, they are to carry out the work of the Spirit. They are to breathe that Spirit upon the chaotic waters of their world. By offering hope, by forgiving, by promoting peace, they transform chaos into cosmos. By demanding justice, by reaching out to the marginalized, by respecting human life from conception to natural death, they change the valley of dead bones into a living, pulsating community. The Eucharist empowers them to breathe the Spirit in these and similar ways. The Eucharist is not only a facet of ongoing creation, but its stimulus as well.

As noted earlier, the celebration of the Eucharist on Sunday recalls Jesus' resurrection from the dead. Against the background of ongoing creation, however, the Eucharist assumes an even greater context since it finds a conspicuous place in God's overall creative plan. God, who created in the beginning and continued to create in Israel's history, demonstrates that creative energy on a larger scale by raising his Son on Easter. While according to the author of John, the resurrection brings God's creative designs to completion, the Eucharist suggests that creation is still ongoing and, to that extent, the work of the Creator must ever be renewed. By coming together for the Eucharist on Sunday, believers call upon God to continue to renew his work of creation. The presence of the eucharistic Jesus reminds them that the drama of salvation has not yet concluded. The Eucharist sustains hope in that final act of creation.

REVIEW AND/OR DISCUSSION QUESTIONS

1. *What situation does the creation story of Genesis 1:1—2:4a address?*

2. *What is the dilemma faced by humans in Psalm 8?*

3. *What are the elements of ongoing creation in Jesus' baptism (Mark 1:10)?*

4. *How does ongoing creation relate to the celebration of the Eucharist?*

CHAPTER NINE

Revelation

INITIAL THOUGHTS

The etymology of "revelation" is a Latin root meaning to pull back the veil or covering, hence to disclose. While this offers some clues, the Dogmatic Constitution on Divine Revelation from Vatican II develops this basic notion of communication. It states that in the plan of salvation, deeds and words comprise a unity. God's deeds in history confirm the reality expressed by the words. In turn, the words clarify the meaning of God's deeds. Revelation, therefore, does not imply fully packaged concepts dropped from the heavens, but a blending of divine deeds and words that disclose God's will and the destiny of humanity.

Revelation involves a process and several components. First, God communicates both himself and his involvement with humanity in creation that signals his wisdom, power, and love. Second, God reveals his vision for humanity in history, beginning with the call of Abraham (see Genesis 12:1–3). God directs and guides this vision with the role of Moses and his choice of a people, namely Israel. In the history of that singular people, God communicates in a special way through the prophets who deliver both his criticizing and energizing message. Third, God reaches the high point of his revelatory power by sending his Son, Jesus. In the words of the Letter to the Hebrews, "In times past, God spoke in partial and various ways to our ancestors and through the prophets; in these last days, he spoke to us through a son" (1:1–2). As God's personal revelation, Jesus tells humanity who God is, specifying the intimate relationship existing between the Father and himself.

For many, the word "mystery" implies something utterly incomprehensible or impenetrable. One may think of a mystery novel and thus wait until the very end to have everything unraveled and resolved. Surprisingly, while a dimension of something secret still remains, mystery also unfolds the quality of the known and hence provides awe and wonder, and not merely ignorance. The author of 1 Timothy states that "the mystery of our religion is great" but summarily quotes an early Christian hymn in which Jesus was revealed in the flesh and proclaimed among gentiles (3:16). Pope Paul VI captures this mingling of wonder, communication, and elusiveness when he identifies mystery as a reality imbued with the hidden presence of God.

Revelation and prayer go hand-in-glove. In the process of

revealing, God discloses himself, his will, and his plan of salvation. Revelation impacts the believer and sets up a dialogue in which God and the believer must interact. While revelation involves the communication of who God is and what is expected of the believer, it involves much more. In the immortal words of Abraham Heschel, the purpose of speech is to inform, but the purpose of prayer is to partake. In prayer, the believer can interact on a variety of levels. Such include awe and wonder, praise and petition, worship and obeisance. A life without prayer is not a fully human life. Only prayer coupled with obedience maintains a vibrant, healthy give-and-take between Revealer and believer.

BIBLICAL BACKGROUND

Psalm 19 is a hymn or psalm of descriptive praise that consists of two different but complementary psalms. In the first psalm (vv. 1–7), the accent lies on the beauty of God's achievement in creation. "The heavens declare the glory of God; the firmament proclaims the works of his hands" (v. 2). The heavens and the firmament seem to be personified spaces, while day and night (v. 3) function as personified periods of time. In verses 4–5, the earth serves as the great audience hall that listens to their discourse and acknowledges God's revelation in creation.

Like her ancient Near Eastern neighbors, Israel emphasized the role of wisdom in life. Wisdom embraced a wide range of meanings: labor skills, counseling expertise, general cleverness, and rules of conduct expressed especially in proverbs, academic expertise, and the like. However, Israel eventually concluded that such a priceless reality as wisdom did not belong solely to the human world. Rather, God had to possess this invaluable commodity in the greatest way possible. To the question about the origin of wisdom, Israel responded, "God understands the way to her; it is he who knows her place" (Job 28:23).

Israel also believed that God constituted a creature, Lady Wisdom, the personification of wisdom, to function as his agent in revealing this precious gift. As God's assistant in the plan of creation, she takes delight in the human race (Proverbs 8:31). As his agent, Lady Wisdom stands at the gates of the city and cries out, "To you, O people, I call; my appeal is to you mortals. You naive ones, gain prudence, you fools, gain sense" (Proverbs 8:4–5). Communication of God's will is her highest priority. Against this background, one can readily appreciate Paul's perception of Jesus as "the wisdom of God" (1 Corinthians 1:24).

The prophets occupy a special place in communicating God's word to Israel, whether for better or worse. The Bible borrows from the ancient Near East in depicting God as assisted by a divine council for the purposes of making decisions or recommendations. Prophets function either as members of such a council or as eavesdroppers on its deliberations. In Amos 3:7, for example, God executes no plan without first communicating it to his prophets. In a famous attack on false prophets, Jeremiah raises this question: "Now, who has stood in the council of the LORD, to see him and to hear his word" (23:18)? He concludes that, if such prophets had been privy to the divine council, they would have announced God's will to the people and so provoked their repentance (23:22).

In the New Testament there are two significant uses of the Greek root "to reveal"/"revelation" that impact no lesser figures than Peter and Paul. At Caesarea Philippi, when Jesus asks his disciples about his real identity, Peter responds that he is the Messiah, the Son of the living God (Matthew 16:16). Acknowledging Peter's perception, Jesus clarifies its origin. "Flesh and blood has not revealed this to you, but my heavenly Father" (v. 17). Peter's identification of Jesus, therefore, does not stem from purely human resources ("flesh and blood") but from a special insight provided by Jesus' Father. Similarly, Paul confidently asserts that his gospel does not derive from purely human resources but enjoys a unique origin. "It came through a revelation of Jesus Christ" (Galatians 1:12). In these instances, God elects a special mode of communication that sets Peter and Paul apart.

Elsewhere, Paul speaks about this revelation in the context of wisdom versus foolishness and the demand for signs. "For Jews demand signs and Greeks look for wisdom, but we proclaim Christ crucified..." (1 Corinthians 1:22–23). God's plan for humanity that was hidden for so long is now revealed in the crucified one. Paul sees himself as a steward who shares this profound insight with his communities (1 Corinthians 4:1: "stewards of the mysteries of God"). The author of Colossians interprets Paul's thought by underlining the plan's inclusion of the gentiles: "God chose to make known the riches of the glory of this mystery..." (1:27).

The Gospels elaborate how Jesus communicates the kingdom's message through his teaching (especially the parables) and his miracles. However, in a passage very reminiscent of the Gospel of John, Matthew and Luke emphasize Jesus' role as revealer. "All things have been handed over to me by my Father. No one knows the Son except the Father, and no one knows the Father except the Son and anyone to whom the Son wishes to reveal him" (Matthew 11:27; also see Luke 10:22).

In this scene, Jesus elects to share the mutual knowledge of Father and Son with his disciples. By means of this revelation, disciples gain access to the intimacy between Father and Son.

It is the Gospel of John, however, that excels in presenting Jesus as God's revelation. The conclusion of the prologue captures this focus: "No one has ever seen God. The only Son, God who is at the Father's side, has revealed him" (1:18). Like Lady Wisdom, Jesus reaches out to humanity and derives pleasure in being in their midst (1:11 and 14). Also like Lady Wisdom, Jesus speaks in a solemn, sacred style. For example, I am the light of the world, the bread of life, the vine, etc. The author of this Gospel reveals God's love by the giving of his only Son (3:16) that reaches its supreme expression in Jesus' self-giving on the cross (12:32). As Jesus testifies at the Last Supper, he has made known his Father's name to his disciples (17:6). As the personal revelation of the Father, Jesus is "the way and the truth and the life" (14:6).

It is appropriate to say a little about the Book of Revelation or the Apocalypse. As a literary genre, it is a form of revelatory literature within a narrative framework in which an other-worldly being communicates a revelation to a human recipient. Abounding in its use of symbolism, this work seeks to reveal a message of hope so that Christians will remain faithful to their calling. It encourages them to accept only Jesus as Lord and reject the imperial cult. To this end, the book pronounces the defeat of the dragon (the embodiment of Roman evil) in heaven, though the battle still rages on earth for believers. To demonstrate that their perseverance will ultimately win out, the author envisions a new heaven and a new earth (21:1–8) along with a vision of the New Jerusalem (21:9—22:5). Far from predicting the end of the world, Revelation/Apocalypse proffers a message of hope for the beleaguered followers of Jesus. Revelation and hope are vitally interconnected.

REFLECTIONS

Although not official teachers in the Church, all believers by reason of their baptism must be committed to communicating the revelation of the Good News. They must absorb that message so deeply that it yearns to be revealed to others. It thereby becomes a contagious and infectious reality that seeks to affect and reorient others. All followers of Jesus are necessarily involved in this great enterprise of communication that serves as a synonym of sorts for revelation. Such communication does not necessarily require a bully pulpit or street-corner preaching. Essentially, it demands incorporating God's message into one's entire person and then demonstrating it, especially through example. Thus, believers who truly care for others reveal that God is indeed love.

Another facet of this revelation is the prophetic role. Owing to their baptism, believers are heralded as prophets as well as priests and kings/queens. Because of their confirmation, they are challenged to speak to unwilling audiences. In their prophetic roles, they do not focus on the prediction of the future. Prophecy is fundamentally speaking on behalf of another, in this case God. In their criticizing mode, prophets do not hesitate to tell it the way it really is. In their energizing mode, prophets tell it the way it can be and thereby reveal a message of hope. In insisting on the demands of social justice, respect for all human life from conception to natural death, honesty in public policy, etc., these prophets tell it the way it really is. In counseling the despairing, assisting the handicapped, promoting Special Olympics, etc., these prophets tell it the way it can be. Prophetic ministry and revelation are intimately linked.

Take time to smell the roses! Believers must heed the opening line of Psalm 19: "The heavens declare the glory of God." The marvels of the natural world are still worthy of both the attention and admiration of believers. They proclaim the power, majesty, and inventiveness of the Creator. Unfortunately, given the fast-paced modern world, believers have to make a concerted effort to slow down and enjoy the beauty of creation. After all, to respect creation is to respect the Creator. To experience awe and wonder at the delicate but powerful feats of the Creator is to break out in praise. "You spread out the heavens like a tent; setting the beams of your chambers upon the waters" (Psalm 104:2–3).

There is no absolute norm for prayer in the Scriptures. However, the Book of Psalms offers something of a guide with its ups and downs. Hymns or psalms of descriptive praise recite God's ongoing care or provision. For instance, see Psalm 103:13: "As a father has compassion on his children, so the Lord has compassion on those who fear him." At such times, one can also pray psalms of trust or confidence, as in Psalm 23:1: "The Lord is my shepherd; there is nothing I lack." In times of disorientation, namely when calamity strikes and doubts about God's fidelity surface, the believer can pray the biblical lament and challenge God, as in Psalm 22:1: "My God, my God, why have you abandoned me?" In times of reorientation or new orientation, namely when the God of surprises overcomes despair and hopelessness with something new and unexpected, the believer can pray a psalm of thanksgiving or declarative praise, as in Psalm 30:12: "You changed my mourning into dancing; you took off my sackcloth and clothed me with gladness." The Book of Psalms fosters ongoing interaction between revealer and believer.

THE EUCHARIST

In the Bread of Life discourse in John 6, the author presents Jesus as God's revelation. He is the true bread from heaven who has perfected the former bread, namely the manna in the desert (v. 58). Here the Eucharist becomes the place where believers come to eternal life. The broken flesh of Jesus and his spilled blood challenge believers to accept or reject Jesus as the Father's revelation (vv. 56–58). To accept is to gain life, to reject is to lose life (vv. 53–54). To celebrate the Eucharist is to proclaim the revelation that Jesus is the Father's definitive expression of genuine life.

The eucharistic dimensions of John 6, with emphasis on Jesus' self-giving and subsequent eternal life, form a link to Jesus' revelation in his dialogue with Nicodemus in John 3. In verse 14, Jesus states unequivocally that he must be lifted up, that is, his death on the cross will become his exaltation. In verse 15, Jesus states that those who accept this revelation will gain eternal life. Verse 16 reveals the Father's love in the sending of Jesus: "For God so loved the world that he gave his only Son, so that everyone who believes in him might not perish but might have eternal life." The Eucharist captures in a truly compelling way the revelation of the Father's love in the gift of the Son.

The Eucharist reveals the Christian community as the body of Christ (1 Corinthians 12:1–31). As that body, the Church reveals the risen Lord as still active and present among humanity, especially when celebrating the Eucharist. Upon gathering for the Eucharist, the Church offers thanks to God in the Spirit for what Jesus has achieved by his death and resurrection. It also recommits itself to communicating that achievement to the entire world by doing what Jesus did, namely giving oneself in love. The Eucharist symbolizes in a most profound way Jesus' revelation of what it really means to love.

Presence, not absence, makes the heart grow fonder. "This is my body" (Mark 14:22) and "this is my blood" (14:24) tell believers that Jesus continues to be present under the appearances of bread and wine. In the Eucharist, Jesus confirms his commitment to remain with the Church until his Second Coming. The Eucharist, therefore, reveals in a most compelling way Jesus' resolve never to abandon his followers. Jesus reveals himself as the ultimate expression of fidelity.

The revelation in the Eucharist of the Father's love and the Son's submission in death must move believers to emulate this love and obeisance in their seemingly ordinary lives. By reaching out to the unchurched, by alleviating the pain and anguish of others, etc., they hand on the revelation in the Eucharist. By eating the bread and drinking the cup, they become food and drink for others. In this way, the revelation in the Eucharist does not become unknowable but the source of new life and energy. The Eucharist enables believers to share the revelation, the mystery of faith they proclaim in the breaking of the bread.

REVIEW AND/OR DISCUSSION QUESTIONS

1. *How does Psalm 19 understand God's different ways of revealing?*

2. *How does Lady Wisdom function as an agent of God's revelation in Proverbs 8?*

3. *How does the Gospel of John depict Jesus as revealer?*

4. *How does the Bread of Life discourse in John 6 present Jesus as God's revelation?*

CHAPTER TEN

Relatives

INITIAL THOUGHTS

Insistence on community flies in the face of modern society, where rank individualism holds sway. "Me, myself, and I" have become humanity's favorite pronouns, to the detriment of "we, you, and they." Advertisements flaunt the ego factor to the extent that its nonfulfillment must necessarily spell disaster and doom. Even when other persons are considered, it is only insofar as they can meet one's individual needs. This is all a far cry from Walter Brueggemann's perceptive remark of some forty years ago that "we" precedes "me" theologically, chronologically, and logically.

The commonly understood heaven symbol has wreaked havoc on the notion of community or extended family. People tend to think they are going to that place "up there" in single file. To compound matters, heaven is reserved only for their souls, not their bodies. When time for judgment comes, Jesus, they believe, will question them about their individual gains and losses. "Jesus and just me," their *modus vivendi* (manner of living) for all too long, has now become their *modus moriendi* (manner of dying).

Nonetheless, some people still yearn for genuine community in the face of this unbridled individualism. They express this desire when they say, "Let's get together and create community now." There is a certain irony in this wish. It presumes that community does not yet exist, but with their persistent efforts, it will come into existence. Paul would certainly chide such a group. He would point out that the community, namely the Christian community, already exists and that by their incorporation into it they belong to something greater than themselves. Instead of creating community, individuals are absorbed into an already-existing one.

Emphasis on community must impact one's notion of liturgy. As the official public worship of the Church, liturgy necessarily envisions the faithful coming together as a body to offer praise and thanksgiving to God. While private prayer and devotion have their proper place, liturgy precedes them because of the centrality of community. At worship, therefore, believers are not perceived as isolated individuals "doing their own thing." Rather, they come together as members of an extended family who have common goals and needs. Liturgy without community is a contradiction in terms.

BIBLICAL BACKGROUND

Covenant serves as the foundation of community in the Old Testament. In its widest sense, covenant is a form of relationship. More precisely, it is a relationship in which a moral connection between participants is, first of all, defined and, secondly, affirmed. Exodus 6:7 provides a good example of the covenant formula. "I will take you as my own people, and I will be your God." The Ten Commandments and the other laws at Sinai illustrate what is expected of Israel as covenant partner. In this covenant, Israel is a family that is descended from Abraham, Isaac, and Jacob (Genesis 48:15—49:27). By having a covenantal relationship with God, Israel also has a covenantal relationship with each other. By being bound up with God, Israel is also bound up with all the individual members of his people. To react and interact with God means to react and interact with the entire people.

Elsewhere, the Old Testament captures this covenantal relationship by the use of family titles. Thus the Lord is Israel's father (see Isaiah 63:16 and Jeremiah 3:4). According to Deuteronomy 28:10, Israel also enjoys a special designation: "All the peoples of the earth shall see that the name of the LORD is proclaimed over you." In the Exodus setting, Moses must inform Pharaoh that Israel is the Lord's firstborn son (Exodus 4:22). The Exodus experience itself is grounded in a familial relationship. "When Israel was a child I loved him, out of Egypt I called my son" (Hosea 11:1).

While the Old Testament never calls the God of Israel "mother," the imagery used in several passages is clearly maternal. For example, the covenantal poem in Deuteronomy 32 chides Israel for neglecting the obligations of their relationship. "You were unmindful of the Rock that begot you, you forgot the God who gave you birth" (v. 18). In Isaiah, God feels intense anguish for the exiles and resolves to intervene on their behalf. "Now I cry out like a woman in labor, gasping and panting" (42:14). The maternal concern of God also reveals itself in the miracles of the wilderness wandering. Since supplying food and drink is typically a maternal chore, the God of Israel meets these needs by providing quail and manna (Exodus 16:4–36 and Numbers 11:31–35) as well as water (Exodus 17:1–7 and Numbers 20:2–13). In Numbers, Moses complains to God that he is already overburdened with solving the people's problems and, therefore, Israel's mother must intervene. "Was it I who conceived all this people? Or was it I who gave them birth..." (11:12)? Maternal instincts require God to act now.

In the Gospels, Jesus uses kinship language to designate his disciples. In Mark 3:31–35, Jesus' mother and brothers (his physical family) are standing outside, asking for him (vv. 31–32). When informed of their presence, he poses the question about the criterion for discipleship: "Who are my mother and [my] brothers" (v. 33)? Glancing at the disciples sitting around him, Jesus designates them as his mother and his brothers (v. 34). Blood relationship, therefore, does not constitute one a disciple. Rather, "whoever does the will of God is my brother and sister and mother" (v. 35). Here kinship language serves to identify those who follow him.

In Luke 14:1–24, a Sabbath meal at the home of a leading Pharisee becomes the setting for considering the attitudes of participants toward one another. It consists of three components: (1) the cure of a man with dropsy (vv. 1–6), (2) sayings regarding the proper conduct of guests (vv. 7–14), and (3) the parable of the great dinner (vv. 15–24). In the cure of the man with dropsy on the Sabbath, Jesus addresses the issue of community by asking if it is lawful to heal on the Sabbath. To make his point, Jesus implicitly criticizes his opponents for their lack of compassion for a fellow human being with this question: "Who among you, if your son or ox falls into a cistern, would not immediately pull him out on the sabbath day" (v. 5)? In the sayings about the appropriate behavior, occupying the last place assures the guest of a position of honor (vv. 7–11). In a world where one invites only those who can reciprocate the favor at a later date, Jesus urges inviting the poor, the crippled, the lame, and the blind, namely people who cannot return the favor (vv. 12–14). In the parable of the great dinner, the invitees, for a variety of reasons, have a change of plans. This forces the host to invite the outcasts (the poor, the crippled, the blind, and the lame). When this strategy fails to fill the available room, the host opts to invite those on the roads and in the lanes (vv. 15–24). In the end, the Sabbath meal has to do with the recognition of community. Specifically it deals with family members who will share fellowship with Jesus at the final messianic banquet.

In Matthew's famous judgment of the nations (25:31–46), the evangelist spells out the criteria for salvation and condemnation. Basically, he proposes a theology of disguises. Thus, salvation hinges on discovering Jesus in the helpless and marginalized (the hungry, thirsty, strangers, naked, sick, and imprisoned). In turn, condemnation results from not finding Jesus in such people. In verse 40, Jesus reveals his theology of disguises by means of kinship language. "I say to you, whatever you did for one of these least brothers of mine (although a masculine noun in Greek, the term also includes sisters), you did for me."

In Acts, Luke narrates the conversion of Saul/Paul no less than three times (9:1–19, 22:6–16, and 26:12–18). On his way to Damascus to continue his persecution of Christians, Saul/Paul experiences the transforming vision of the risen Lord. Although Luke does not use kinship language in describing Jesus' relationship to the persecuted, he still captures the intimate bond between them and Jesus. "Saul, Saul, why are you persecuting me" (9:4)? After a request for the speaker's identity comes the clarification: "I am Jesus, whom you are persecuting" (9:5). Jesus thus clearly identifies with his followers.

In 1 Corinthians, Paul refers to his addressees no less than twenty times as "brothers and sisters." In fact, this familial address sounds almost like a refrain. By means of such language, Paul hopes to counteract the divisiveness of this fragmented community. Their divisions over a variety of issues contradict their supposed family unity. For example, in 6:1–8, Paul takes up the matter of lawsuits among fellow Christians. He asks whether there is not someone wise enough in the community to decide between one brother and another (v. 5). The irony of the situation is that one brother takes another brother to court and indeed before unbelievers. For Paul, bonds of kinship should keep family members from making their squabbles public in the presence of an unbelieving judge.

REFLECTIONS

Covenant offers identity. As Israel was grounded in the Lord, the Church is grounded in Jesus through his passion-death-resurrection experience. Hence, the identity process begins outside human beings. It starts with the one who possesses the ability to call them forth and enable them to reach their full potential as family members. To be identified as one of those family members is nothing less than to receive an enormous gift. In turn, this gift-giving envisions the ministry of thanksgiving. Family members must always remember to say thank you.

The expression of gratitude to this giver of gifts does not exhaust one's obligations as a family member. Some thirty years ago, Walter Brueggemann wrote that, in the Bible, person means belonging with, belonging to, and belonging for. The family member, precisely as person, must belong not only to, with, and for God but to, with, and for other family members. Believers cannot have it only one way, namely to, with, and for God. The community must also share in this trio of belonging. To accept God as the head of the family means to accept his family members as one's own. Exclusiveness has never been the family tradition.

In 1 Thessalonians, Paul expresses his deep affection for this community by calling them brothers and sisters no less than fourteen times. Clearly the term articulates Paul's love for the Thessalonians and, in turn, their own mutual family relationship. In recalling their initial conversion, Paul adroitly describes what constitutes them a Christian family of believers in 1:5–8. The first ingredient is the acceptance of the gospel message as preached by Paul and his companions. "Our gospel did not come to you in word alone, but also in power and in the holy Spirit..." (v. 5). The second ingredient is the demonstration of that message in daily life, "...imitators of us and of the Lord...so that you became a model for all the believers" (vv. 6-7). For Paul, these two ingredients belong inexorably together. Hence, it is not sufficient to hear the gospel message. Believers must also complement it with the genuineness of their Christian lives. To belong to this family means to honor the family tradition and its code of honor, namely fidelity day in and day out.

Family awareness should lead believers to recognize and respect the conscience of their sisters and brothers. At Corinth a portion of meat sacrificed to idols in pagan temples went on sale in the public market (1 Corinthians 8:1–13). The question arose whether Christians could eat such meat in good conscience. The stronger members of the community felt that it was perfectly lawful to eat such meat, since idols really did not exist. The weaker members, however, were scandalized by this practice and insisted on not eating such meat because it was offered to idols. Given this division, Paul wants the stronger members of the community to make sure that their liberty does not become a stumbling block for the weaker members (v. 9). He also reminds the stronger members that Christ died for the weaker ones (v. 11). Appealing to the family relationship between both groups and Jesus, he draws this conclusion: "When you sin in this way against your brothers, and wound their consciences, weak as they are, you are sinning against Christ" (v. 12). The family bond thus takes precedence over personal freedom.

THE EUCHARIST

While Matthew 26:28 and Mark 14:24 present Jesus as saying over the cup, "This is my blood of the covenant," Luke 22:20 and 1 Corinthians 11:25 offer a variation: "This cup is the new covenant in my blood." Matthew and Mark intend a reference to the blood of the covenant rite in Exodus 24:8. Without excluding that reference, Luke and Paul have enlarged the scene with an allusion to Jeremiah 31:31. In that passage, Jeremiah speaks of a new covenant that the Lord will make with the house of Israel and the house of Judah. In this new covenant, God will put his Torah within them and write it on their hearts. The celebration of the Eucharist, therefore, recalls the bond that now exists between Jesus and the Christian community. The Eucharist does not establish a purely private relationship between two parties, namely Jesus and the individual. Rather, the Eucharist envisions a community of believers coming together for a common goal. Worshippers eat the loaf and drink the cup in a family setting.

In 1 Corinthians 11:33–34, Paul appeals in these words to his fractured Corinthian Christians: "Therefore, my brothers, when you come together to eat, wait for one another. If anyone is hungry, he should eat at home." In an effort to counter the fractious behavior in Corinth, Paul recommends conduct based on the family relationship of the participants. The Corinthians should treat each other as family members. Paul drives home this same point a few verses earlier. He remarks that "for anyone who eats and drinks without discerning the body, eats and drinks judgment on himself" (v. 29). While some interpret "body" as the Eucharist in contradistinction to common food, Paul most likely is speaking of the Christian community as "body" since verses 27–34 provide the solution to the problem of the community in verses 17–22. In the latter verses, Paul criticizes the Corinthians because they do not act as a body (see 10:17) but, on the contrary, engage in self-serving, individualistic practices. Hence, for Paul, all those who wish to celebrate the Body and Blood of the Lord must realize that they must act as a body, namely a unified community. Anything less is a sham.

Luke 14:1–24, although it does not focus specifically on the Eucharist, does raise the question of the Eucharist and community. By its very nature, the Eucharist is the sacrament of unity. It demands a truly ecumenical vision in that the less-than-beautiful people (the poor, the crippled, the lame, and the blind) feel at home as members of the same family. The Eucharist powerfully reminds all participants that, in sharing the Body and Blood of Jesus, they symbolize their common bond as his extended family. This requires all participants to dismiss all arrogance and elitism. They must welcome each other as equals, financial status and personal honor notwithstanding. In the mind of Jesus, the Eucharist and unity are inseparable.

The Eucharist without genuine community is simply not the Eucharist. In eating the loaf and drinking the cup, believers must recognize their family identity. As sisters and brothers of Jesus, they come together because they share a common bond and destiny. Far from being isolated individuals, they are a tightly knit family that recalls Jesus' self-giving and, implicitly at least, seeks to emulate him. The dying of Jesus must become an overpowering symbol that leads them to honor the family name and the family code of conduct. In offering a sign of peace to each other, for example, believers must go beyond expressing a quaint wish for a cessation of hostilities. Through their gesture they commit themselves to taking steps to preserve and, if need be, enhance the well-being of their family members.

REVIEW AND/OR DISCUSSION QUESTIONS

1. *How does the biblical notion of covenant affect one's relationship with God and other covenant members?*

2. *What kind of language describes Israel's relationship to God and God's relationship to Israel?*

3. *According to Matthew 25:31–46, how does Jesus regard the marginalized?*

4. *How does Paul understand the relationship between the Eucharist and community in 1 Corinthians 11:17–34?*